An Ambiguous Journey
to the City

In this book, Ashis Nandy tells the story of an apparently
territorial journey—the one between the village and the city—to
capture some of the core fantasies and anxieties of the Indian
civilization in the past hundred years. He contends that the
decline of the village in the creative imagination of Indians in
recent decades has altered the meaning of this journey drastically.
And that even the true potentialities of Indian cosmopolitanism
and urbanity cannot be realized without rediscovering the myth
of the village.

Rich in theoretical insights and written in an engaging style,
this book will delight scholars across disciplines as much as
general readers concerned with the psychology and politics
of culture.

Ashis Nandy is ICSSR National Fellow, associated with the
Centre for the Study of Developing Societies, Delhi.

An Ambiguous Journey to the City

The Village and Other Odd Ruins of the Self in the Indian Imagination

ASHIS NANDY

OXFORD
UNIVERSITY PRESS

OXFORD
UNIVERSITY PRESS

YMCA Library Building, Jai Singh Road, New Delhi 110 001

Oxford University Press is a department of the University of Oxford. It furthers the
University's objective of excellence in research, scholarship, and education
by publishing worldwide in

Oxford   New York

Auckland Cape Town Dar es Salaam Hong Kong Karachi Kuala Lumpur
Madrid Melbourne Mexico City Nairobi New Delhi Shanghai Taipei Toronto

With offices in

Argentina Austria Brazil Chile Czech Republic France Greece Guatemala
Hungary Italy Japan Poland Portugal Singapore South Korea Switzerland
Thailand Turkey Ukraine Vietnam

Oxford is a registered trademark of Oxford University Press
in the UK and in certain other countries

Published in India by Oxford University Press, New Delhi

First published 2001
Oxford India Paperbacks 2007
Second impression 2009

ISBN-13: 978-0-19-568397-4
ISBN-10: 0-19-568397-8

Typeset in Adobe Garamond
by Guru Typograph Technology, New Delhi 110 045
Printed in India by De-Unique, New Delhi 110 018
Published by Oxford University Press
YMCA Library Building, Jai Singh Road, New Delhi 110 001

To the memory of D.R. Nagaraj (1953–98), literary theorist, classical scholar, cultural critic, political activist, colleague, friend, and the most remarkable Indian intellectual of his generation that I met. He embodied the creative vigour of non-colonized, non-Brahminic, vernacular India, even when he did not write about it.

Preface

This book is an expanded version of the first series of Jerusalem Lectures in Indian Civilization, given at Jerusalem in December 1997 under the title of 'Imaginary Journeys'. It tells the story of India's ambivalent affair with the modern city through the myth of the journey between the village and the city and the changes that myth has undergone. The lectures were at the initiative of the Hebrew University and they remain associated in my memory with the fascinating intellectual exchanges I had with psychoanalysts, psychotherapists, philosophers, social and political theorists, anthropologists and, above all, David Shulman, the moving spirit behind the series. This book reflects that cultural context in its concern with up-rooting, mega-deaths and, particularly, the fear of the self that has turned the urban–industrial vision into a patented cure for every ontological insecurity and the last word in human civilization—not merely in Europe in the 1930s and India in the 1940s, but also in Israel and India in the 1990s.

I write these words a few months after India and Pakistan have exploded a series of nuclear devices. In India at least, the new generation of well-educated, urbane élite has been bristling for years at the limits imposed by the legacy of the country's freedom movement on hard-eyed political 'realism'. In the fiftieth year of the execution of Mohandas Karamchand Gandhi by an assassin wedded to such realism, this élite has now finally shed the cultural and ethical encumbrances associated with his name. In place of these encumbrances have come the grim instrumentality and rationality of the rootless, deracinated, massified, urban middle classes, and a set of civic virtues that these classes believe will fight the romanticism sired by the region's nasty, sterile, rustic past. These classes are willing to mortgage their children's future to dedicated necrophiles in order to ensure that the country does not remain mired in that past. To the psychologically homeless person living in an adversarial neighbourhood, the fantasy of the devastated homes of neighbours does not always seem repellent. They may even be a part of normal political cost calculation.

In the whole southern world, the beckoning magic of the new colonial metropolis frames the mythic journey to the city. Such a city vends a dream of total freedom for the individual and the reasoning self, both organized around an ego so autonomous that it yields agency to nothing outside itself. In the official ideologies of conformity and dissent floating around in post-colonial societies, the journey to the city is a journey from a self buffeted by primordial passions and an authoritarian conscience—the village is seen as the repository of these—to a self identified with fully autonomous ego functions.

This dream of the city usually comes with a cultivated forgetfulness about the violent record of the last hundred years, a record which shows the complicity of the secular city of citizenship, civility, and civic virtues with a particularly ruthless form of self-indulgent, unrestrained, asocial individualism. Such individualism shelters at its centre not the classical, potentially emancipatory Freudian ego, but an overly protected gilded ego that has only apparently shed its encumbrances. For it is now buffeted by another kind of primordiality—the crackpot rationality and objectivity in which the modern public self has specialized, and with which the seemingly autonomous Freudian ego of the western *Homo psychologicus* seems to be deceitfully in league. The imagined city in South Asia symbolizes the belated attempts of defeated civilizations to break into the hard 'realism' of the world of winners where, to stretch the metaphor of Ivan Illich, specialist skills in hydrology and water management transform the waters of dream into a scarce commodity called H_2O.

The attempts at a controlled 'regression' to the village in the South Asian imagination, then, can be read as a form of play with visions that chalk out another possible point of departure for the city. It consecrates the hope—as in the case of Gandhi's triumphant march to Dandi through the villages of Gujarat in the 1920s, or his magical walk through the riot-affected villages of Noakhali in East Bengal in 1946–7—that the city of the future will be more modest and sceptical about its privileged access to realism, its social-evolutionary edge over other lifestyles, its monopoly on multiculturalism and creative individualism. As some of the most urbane thinkers of South Asia have recognized during the last hundred years, the 'return' to the village from the city is often a search for an alternative cosmopolitanism. That cosmopolitanism has a place for the humble vernacular, often incompatible with any iconography of the nation-state, with the compulsions of a global market, and with the demands of a global knowledge industry. What Freud said about war, we can say with minor adjustments about the imagined village that figures in the following pages. With the recovery of the village in the South Asian imaginary, the cities of the region might become interesting again, and we may rediscover their 'full content'. That recovery has also been the concern of thinkers, writers, and activists who define the underground of contemporary civic culture—from William Blake to Henry David Thoreau to the defiant movements for alternatives that plague global capitalism today—the way dysentery once plagued Europe's triumphant civilizing missions in the tropics.

Makarand Paranjape has reminded us recently that crosscultural travel, when not a pilgrimage, is often encased in a neocolonial hierarchy. In our times, only some have the prerogative of travelling to other peoples and lands and reporting on them. Contemporary travel presumes the Dostoyevskian opposition between the anthropologists and the subjects of anthropological enquiry. Journey as a metaphor, however, can also be a way of bearing witness: psychogeographically, it is almost always an expedition to the borders of the self. Al Beruni's journey to India was not so much a one-sided, Columbian discovery of India as a dialogue of civilizations in which the stranger mirrored the self and the self mirrored the stranger. By trying to understand the stranger in the stranger's terms, he not merely confronted his own self but also extended its borders. At this plane, Al Beruni's account of his journey was a play on the double meaning of reflection. His work became a testimony to forms of consciousness to which a philosopher–mystic like Jalaluddin Rumi, not enamoured of terrestrial journeys and clear self–other differences, would have been no stranger. We live in an age of testimony, some have claimed. Perhaps we do, but that testimony should encompass not merely the experience of organized mass violence based on self–other differences in our times. It should also pay homage to the often unheroic, everyday ability to negotiate these differences and the resistance that ability offers to mass violence. To pay that homage, we are obliged to stand witness to the many lost worlds of culture and culturally-based systems of knowledge that have been proclaimed obsolete and, along with the millions of their living practitioners, exported to the past with a remarkable intellectual sleight of hand. So much so that references to these living cultures and to the sufferings and indignities of the millions who live with these cultures are seen as a romantic time travel to the past.

I have finished writing these words sitting in Cochin, a bustling, addictive, medieval city that retains almost nothing of its pre-colonial past in structures and architecture, but still bears the stamp of its distinctive, deviant cosmopolitanism. In Cochin's version of civic virtues, strangers, whom we like to call 'others' these days, can be disliked but not eliminated; indeed they have to be given the right to dislike *you* without nurturing annihilating passions within themselves or in you. Cochin shows that in many cultures the self can be incomplete without its distinctive notselves; indeed, it is partly defined by these not-selves. What looks like a possibility in the future, the city seems to proclaim, may lie scattered or hidden at the margins today, making the futurist's search a disguised self-exploration in the present. Cochin shows that the journey to homelessness is not yet complete in South Asia.

Cochin also suggests that in South Asia the cultural psychology of space usually ends up as a political psychology of time. As the region's obstreperous cultural diversity has become a political liability in the age of globalized civility, anxieties about the region's persisting cultural 'backlog' have grown. Modern India's response has been a heavy-handed use of the theory of progress as a new psychological defence: its job is to index the unknown and the strange as a new set of the anachronistic and the retrogressive. Gradually, whatever in contemporary India is distant from or incongruent with our favourite intellectual categories has become disposable; it is repackaged as history and banished to the past. We talk of living communities and systems of knowledge struggling to survive now as if we were talking of the distant past. Perhaps in the entire postcolonial world, the 'dream work' of creative imagination establishes an easier convertibility between time and space to turn all psychogeographical journeys into psychopolitical ones. These lectures, which began as a mythography of journey in the Indian imaginary, have imperceptibly changed their course to become a political reconstruction of the passions invested in journeys to and from the city.

A word on the organization of this book. Its first section deals with the vicissitudes of the metaphor of journey, especially the imagination of the hero as it intersects with the imagined city. The second and third sections profile the hero as he negotiates the journey from the village to the city and from the city to the village and show that, in doing so, he has to walk into the interiors of his self and dredge its resources to cope with the changing landscape of South Asia. Both journeys end up as doomed expeditions into a self that has partly become another country. The last section deals with the violence of 1946–8, in which the independent states of India and Pakistan were born. It is the story of a psychopatho-logical journey from a poisoned village and the splintering of the self in a self-annihilating city. To speak with Christopher Lasch, when everyday life becomes an exercise in survival, 'selfhood becomes a kind of luxury . . . Selfhood implies a personal history, family, a sense of place. Under siege, the self contracts to a defens-ive core, armed against adversity. Emotional equilibrium demands a minimal self, not the imperial self of yesteryear.' The last section of the book is, on one plane, a story of the abridgement of the self and the dissolution of the hero.

Parts of the first section draw upon an informal presentation made at a *samaskriti shivira* or workshop on culture studies, Ninasam, Heggodu, Karnataka over 15–28 October 1994. I am grateful to the participants and organizers of the course, particularly M.N. Srinivas and U.R. Anantha Murthy, for the excellent, animated discussion that followed the lecture. The first section is also partly based upon the Tagore–Yeats lecture of 1998, given at the Nehru Centre, London. The comments of some listeners, particularly Indranath Chaudhuri and William Radice, have influ-enced the present version. The second section bases itself on a paper written for *Understanding and Perspective: Workshop on Popular Indian Culture*, organised by Chris Pinney and Rachel Dwyer at the School of Oriental and African Studies, University of London, 19–21 June 1995. I have gained much from the comments of the participants, especially the detailed critical responses of Rachel Dwyer. Mrinal Dutta Chaudhuri was the first to suggest the theme—a 'psychological autopsy' of Pramathesh Barua—and to put me in touch with Debolina Barua, without whose help this section just could not have been written.

The third section owes much to help given by Mrinal Sen. It was first presented at a public lecture in 1996, organized by Murari Ballal of the Department of Humanities, University of Manipal. The last section draws upon a public lecture given at Bangalore to honour the memory of D.R. Nagaraj soon after his death in August 1998. Parts of it are based on a study of the experiences of and resistance to Partition violence, done at the Committee for Cultural Choices by, among others, Chandrika Parmar, Anindita Mukhopadhyaya, Meenakshi Verma, Imtiaz Ahmed, Nandita Bhavnani, Rehan Ansari, Aleeka, and Amena Mohsin. I am grateful to them and to the Catholic Relief Services, which partly supported the study. An earlier version of the section was written for *Postcolonial Studies*. Incidentally, the term 'holocaust' has a double meaning in this section. It derives both from the literature on modern genocide and from a rough translation of the concept of *pralaya* which underpins the stories of many victims of Partition violence.

The book as a whole has gained much from the comments of D.R. Nagaraj, Giri Deshingkar, and some of the listeners at Jerusalem and the index from the detailed work of Meenakshi Verma. The idea of a book centring around the cultural psychology of the city was Ravi Sundaram's. I doubt whether he will approve of the product, though.

Delhi
July 1999

1

The Journey to the Past as a Journey into the Self

The Remembered Village and the Poisoned City

'It is not binding on us to undertake the journey'
Manohar Wakode

The nineteenth century in Europe was an age of arrogance. The values of the Enlightenment had seeped into popular consciousness and qualities earlier associated with the divine had come to be associated with secular human intervention in nature, culture and society—thanks to a dramatic growth in the capacity to intervene. Complete knowledge, omnipresence and total power now seemed within human grasp. The Victorian social style, with its distinctive touch of interpersonal withdrawal and phlegmatic, if slightly diffident, Puritanism was built on understatement and innuendo. It became a good cover for the arrogance, though it never fully hid it.[1]

With arrogance came ornate psychological defences that justified new forms of dominance; these forms began to look like

[1] I am, of course, following Carl Jung, generalizing the idea of the Victorian era from a historical phase in Britain to a cultural–psychological state in Europe. C.G. Jung, 'Sigmund Freud in His Historical Setting', in Frank Cioffi (ed.), *Freud: Modern Judgement* (London: Macmillan, 1973), pp. 49–56; see esp. pp. 49–50.

natural by-products of Europe's new self-confidence. Thus, European imperialism, already the main political–economic means of intervention in the world, became less obsessed with outright plunder and the need to Christianize the savage world; it began to develop subtler, more secular, social-evolutionary theories to bolster its claim to a civilizing mission. The occupation of distant lands and dominance over strangers now imposed more onerous responsibilities on the conquerors. They had to see themselves as part of an inevitable, historical movement towards a future defined by European progressive thinkers. These thinkers were eager to preside over the fate of millions in the non-western world by altering diverse ideas of a desirable society. To survive, these ideas had to now fit standardized European visions of a good society, whether conformist or dissenting.[2]

History, as a discipline and form of consciousness, came handy in this exercise. It flattened the pasts of all societies, so that they began to look like so many edited versions of European paganism and/or feudalism. The triumph of the idea of history in the southern world—over other forms of construction or invocation of the past—was ultimately a European triumph. This conquest was not merely over the selves of other societies, but often over Europe's own earlier selves that had stealthily survived into the present, either in Europe or in analogous or parallel forms within other cultures. Europe truly became Europe as we know it today only after it foregrounded the experiences of colonialism and a crypto-Hegelian idea of history within its self-definition. It also then ensured that these became parts of the self-definitions of all defeated civilizations.

These changes led to others. Within the colonial worldview, the victory of history and the theory of progress signalled human

---

[2] For a recent analysis from a different point of view, see David Newsome, *The Victorian World Picture: Perceptions and Introspections in an Age of Change* (New Brunswick, NJ: Rutgers University Press, 1997).

Contents

victory over time and space. When you conquered and dominated distant lands and shaped their futures, you transcended your own temporal and spatial limits. You not only crossed borders outside, you crossed them within.[3] Strange spaces, in the form of distant lands, were converted into familiar time (that is, into earlier historical phases of Europe); and other people's unruly visions of the future were tamed to conform to Europe's own domesticated visions. The sun that faithfully never set over the British Empire also marked the triumph of human will over the limitations imposed by the predictability of everyday life in Britain itself. This was another form of victory over elements of Europe's discarded selves, another form of self-construction and, above all, another form of death-denial that supplanted the existing non-secular modes of ensuring symbolic immorality.

Such radical cultural changes required new symbols around which the new myths of the modern West could accumulate. The nineteenth century therefore saw the emergence and institutional consolidation of a number of major symbols of conquest over space and time. Two of these quickly captured the popular imagination: the museum and the railways. In the museum one journeyed through time to view the unfolding phases of history and culture, usually through the eyes of one's society, nation or state. In the railway train one experienced a journey that connected the near and the distant, the known and the safely transient unknown, the neighbour and the stranger. The train redefined the concepts of a border and a frontier; it captured long-term diachronic changes in a series of snapshot-like changes in landscape and transient human encounters. Even the European fine arts began to show the influence of this new perspective on nature.[4]

[3] Howard Stein (ed.), *Developmental Time, Cultural Space: Studies in Psychogeography* (Norman: University of Oklahoma, 1987), p. 193.

[4] Christopher Pinney notes that in the practice and theory of Western travel, 'as the world entered the modern period, travel became increasingly

At first sight, the museum symbolized the conquest of time and the railway that of space. However, both spilt over their representational boundaries. The museum grew to symbolize not merely mastery over past times and past cultures at home, but also over the diverse pasts and cultures of distant lands. It also became the record of a journey. It rearranged all cultures in a hierarchical, evolutionary order. As you walked through a museum, you paradoxically walked towards your own culture; only Others had to walk away from theirs. The train came to symbolize not merely geographical mobility, but integration and progress, reaching out from the centre to the borders of a society. Both allowed one to travel through vast expanses of time and space, but always left open the option of a quick, safe return.

Between them, the train and the museum defined an era. They were not the greatest technical innovations of their times, but they summed up the psychological profile and the core concerns of the age. Railways and museums captured, for popular imagination in the Victorian age, something of the dominant spirit of global awareness.

Both railways and museums indexed the domestication of time. They were the technological counterparts of epistemic changes in the means of acquiring and legitimating social knowledge in the Victorian world. The prototypical discipline of knowledge in this era was history (the way that in this century it has been economics and may, in the coming century, be informatics). History tames time in a manner that myths, legends and epics do not. In a massified society, it gives certitudes about the past, and, thus, a secular sense of continuity previously ensured only by faith. Once the historical vision entrenches itself as dominant, 'historical truths'

---

systematized and rule-bound.' Christopher Pinney, 'Future Travel: Anthropology and Cultural Distance in an Age of Virtual Reality; or, A Past Seen From a Possible Future.' *Visual Anthropology Review*, Spring 1992, 8(1), pp. 38–55.

acquire an exalted, sacred status; exploitation and violence, for instance, begin to be institutionalized in the name of history rather than faith.

Once introduced on a large scale, the railways did not merely symbolize the conquest of space, as we tend to think. Symbolically, that conquest had been achieved much earlier, and perhaps better, by the great circumnavigators of the globe. The British and French empires had already been established and they consolidated that symbolic achievement before the railways came to criss-cross the world. The railways altered the way the Victorians thought. When children in the last century spoke of the Trans-Siberian Railway, the Orient Express, the Frontier Mail or the Great Indian Peninsular Railway, they did not think so much of destinations as of the experience of travel. Even the American wagon trains represented a life style more than territoriality. They invoked the imagery of the railway compartment as a moving sanctuary. From within the confines of what Wolfgang Sachs calls a 'republic on wheels', the carriers of civilization were offered a stylized view of the shifting landscape, including the dangerous, exotic natives, 'half-savage half-child', and strange flora and fauna passing safely by at a distance. They marked the transition from the traveller as a tired, thirsty, and often-unexpected guest, pilgrim or explorer to the traveller as a spectator and a consumer. The traveller now travelled not because he felt obliged to open up an unknown world to civilization and progress, but because he had the time and the money to vicariously participate in that kind of effort.[5]

---

[5] Railways opened up, therefore—to borrow Wolfgang Sachs' expression—the possibility of consuming landscapes. In such consumption, 'one need not drink the landscape [or the exotic cultures] in great draughts, but here and there as well with the little sips of an epicure abiding in leisure.' *Der Motor-Tourist*, 1929 (9), p. 8; cited in Wolfgang Sachs, *For the Love of the Automobile: Looking Back into the History of Our Desires* (Berkeley: University of California, 1992), p. 153.

The museum was important because, having travelled to distant lands and encountered the strange and the exotic, you felt duty-bound to bring back artefacts that made it possible to transfer and bequeath memories of the journey to impersonal institutions and unknown fellow citizens. These memories had to be shared not so much with one's grandchildren as with those whom one's nation-state defined as compatriots. Museums sorted out these memories. They made the strange esoteric, but not confounding. They made even the past of strangers accessible, transparent and packaged. That past could be safely brought back to civilization for archiving and decent cataloguing. Ahistorical primitives could now make sense to civilization. Their oddities and incomprehensibilities, even their peculiar non-linear concepts of their own past, were ironed out by the scientific stare of the curator. Indeed our geographical journey was thus made more memorable as part of a larger cultural–historical odyssey.

There is another way of summing up the cultural–psychological impact of the metaphors of museums and trains. The former shaped the public imagination of history. History became for the moderns an authoritative museum, passing final judgements, and a substitute for medieval cathedrals. The psychological and mythic underside of history now became a certain sense of order and a theme of return. The train, on the other hand, shaped the Promethean imagery of a hard-earned victory of technology over the overwhelming odds posed by nature and human nature.

If space and time were both seemingly mastered by the end of the nineteenth century—or, if you like, the technology required for such mastery was felt to have been worked out—what now was left for the adventurous? What now remained for those fired by the new self-confidence of Victorian science, for those itching to embark on spatial and temporal journeys pioneered by seers, mystics and artists on the one hand and by circumnavigators of the world on the other? The answer lies in the intellectual style of two of the greatest critical minds of Victorian times. Freud's time-travel was a journey to the past that allowed one to re-enter the present with the trophy of a conquered savage or primitive self. Marx's psycho-geography was a journey to the savage world that allowed one to return with the trophy of conquered futures that promised to remain forever obedient to European social-evolutionist utopias. If Freud's double was the colonial anthropologist, Marx's was the colonial police. By stretching one's imagination, crime fiction can be seen as the popular culture that epitomizes Freud's moral vision (where the individual, either as a gifted criminal or as master sleuth, reigns supreme, and where the removal or correction of the faulty individual becomes the route to the reinstatement of a healthy society or community). Likewise, the popular idea of science fiction seems to sum up the Marxist vision of a predetermined future waiting to be scientifically identified and actualized. In that future, the ultimate hero is not just any human protagonist but the impersonal forces of technology and history, both liberated from 'misuse' by the ungodly.

It is with these vicissitudes of the metaphor of journey that I shall be concerned here. I shall treat the vicissitudes not as an experience that is uniquely Indian, even when they have their moorings in tradition, but as an artefact of Europe's age of arrogance in the tropics and as a register of the changing mythography of South Asian creativity during the last hundred years. It will be my argument that, during the period, certain core concerns and anxieties of Indian civilization have come to be reflected in the journey from the village to the city, and from the city to the village. Travel through space and time, the known and the unknown and, ultimately, the self and the not-self, get subsumed under these two humble forms of journey. As we shall see below, even the great Partition violence in north India, which killed millions during 1946–8, has become intertwined with the idea of the journey between the village and the city.

I

THE POSSIBILITIES OF AN
EPIC JOURNEY

The journey as a trope for growth, learning, the unfolding of personal or collective experience, and for life itself, has been a favourite of philosophers, scholars and mystics in South Asia for centuries. There have even been celebrated journeys into madness and out of it, journeys in self-exploration and self-realization, even journeys into another world—into heaven, hell and the nether world.[6] Only, in South Asia, heaven and hell, sanity and insanity, the self and the other, more often than not spill into each other. Journeys to the strange or the unknown, therefore, usually end up as private voyages to other, less accessible parts of the self. Arjuna in the epic Mahabharata visits the heavens, Bhima enters the nether world, Nachiketa in the Kathopanishad visits hell, and all of them profit from their experiences. Heavens and hells, gods and demons, animals and trees are not outside the human social world or alien intrusions into that world. You can go to heaven and come back, host or fight a god or demon with impunity, speak to a tree or birds in the course of a single day, and resume your normal social life the next morning.[7]

[6] With the decline of the epic in the contemporary West, the metaphor has been picked up and reworked by popular culture. The most memorable uses of the idea of journey have been made not by the mystics or philosophers in the West, but by the likes of Charles Chaplin, the Hollywood Westerns, and futuristic movies like the *Star Wars* series.

[7] For a feel of the texture of divinity within which such oscillations between the sacred and the profane take place, see Ashis Nandy, 'A Report on the Present

Such journeys are probably more difficult in recent centuries. The anthropologist Jit Singh Uberoi claims that, even in pre-colonial times, there already was a qualitative difference between the ideas of journey in Guru Nanak and Guru Gobind Singh. A journey to the latter meant saddling horses and packing food; to the former, a journey was a matter of closing one's eyes. True, even Guru Gobind Singh's terrestrial journey can be remembered in many ways, but the subjective and the objective in such retellings have already become less fluid. They flow into each other less easily.

In both incarnations, the use of the metaphor of journey to theorize about growth, life, or radical long-cycle changes entails some cognitive manoeuvres. First, the remembrance of life as a journey is heavily dependent on the possible or available meanings of life. At the end of the life, the journey through life might look like a long, futile chase or a self-fulfilling struggle to actualize specific values. Either way, life, thus recaptured, can be an intervention in the present. Likewise, a journey through madness may mean one thing to a mystic or an artist and another to a teenage student who shows dissociative reactions to the problems of living. A journey in South Asia need not have a history, in the sense in which we look at history, but it can constitute part of psychoanalyst's case history, which grants human subjectivity a special status. Everything said, while for Victorian England a journey might have been primarily the frame through which others could be seen,[8] for South Asians it has been mainly the frame through which the self can be confronted.

State of Health of the Gods and Goddesses in South Asia', Lecture at the *samskriti shivira* organized by Ninasam, Heggodu, Karnataka, 8–15 October 1995; and published as 'Facing Extermination', in *Manushi*, March–April 1997 (99), pp. 5–19.

[8] Pinney, 'Future Travel', p. 47.

Second, all journeys in the imagination can be summarized or collapsed into moments of imagination. Ernest Becker has calculated the number of chickens, sheep and cows an average human being consumes in an average lifetime. Given that he is talking of living beings, the figures look formidable, even forbidding, more so because he is not preaching vegetarianism, but trying to capture the principle of a journey by flattening it into a moment of time.

If the diachronic can be compressed into the synchronic in the imagination, the reverse should also be possible. Many momentary experiences can be re-imagined as parts of a longer journey. As we shall see later, the violence during the creation of India and Pakistan in 1946–8 has now become, in the South Asian imagination, part of a journey towards a modern nation-state. The idea of such a journey can become an effort to explain away instances of enormous, unnecessary human suffering as necessary sacrifices for a larger cause.

The journey as a pregnant metaphor is most conspicuous in South Asia in the Mahabharata and the Ramayana, two epics organized around the idea of exile. The exiles in these epics are also great voyages. These voyages redefine both the life that has gone on before and the life that might be lived after the journey has been completed. Travel, the Victorians used to say, broadened the mind, but it can also be a play with the past and the future of the self.

Of the two epics, the Ramayana is more loved, but the Mahabharata is the one that underpins the Indian consciousness. It serves as a mythography of the Indian self and, at the same time, as a record of the disowned selves within the culture—the not-selves and anti-selves that contribute to the final definition of the self.[9] Some of the epic's climactic moments are informed by the metaphor of the journey and it ends with one, the *mahaprasthan*, which becomes the final moral comment on the main protagonists, their lives and deeds. It is not easy to use the metaphor in India without drifting into the frame of some version of the Mahabharata.

I shall be concerned here with one particular, apparently territorial, journey—the one that uses the opposition between the village and the city, especially the changing myth of the city, as its nodal point. In the twentieth century Indians—for that matter, all South Asians—have been obsessed with the mythic journey between the village and the city and have used it to organize important aspects of their public consciousness. The journey is mainly from the village to the city, though it sometimes ends with a tragic attempt to return from the city to the village. South Asians have known this journey for centuries. Pilgrimages were always from the mundane village to the city of God and then back to the village. People knew such journeys were hazardous, but they undertook them all the same. The ones who completed the pilgrimage and returned home had a special status in the community. But so had those who fell on the way. A pilgrimage was a play with the boundaries of the self. Even the inability to complete the journey had heroic dimensions.

This journey to the city acquired a different meaning once, in the early nineteenth century, a new kind of city emerged in the region. The new city, usually a presidency town, was a centre of the colonial political economy; it reduced the importance of cities like Varanasi or Ajmer, which were mainly places of pilgrimage, and of cities like Cochin or Calicut, which were centres of trade and offered their own versions of cosmopolitanism. The new city

[9] At least one psychoanalyst has explored the possibility of using the Mahabharata as a theoretical frame for psychoanalytic therapy. Bijoyketu Bose, *Ja Achche Bharate* (Calcutta: Bijoyketu Bose, 1989).

enlarged the scope for a radical and legitimate rejection of the village as that part of one's self which had out-lived its utility. The journey to the city now meant an acceptance of the new city of the mind, which was to be founded on the ruins of an earlier self.

What made the colonial metropolis the pivotal fantasy and counterpoint to the village? The answer lies not in the 'truth' of the city—its demography, social institutions, civic amenities and job opportunities—but in its 'virtual reality' and mythic status. The structural explanations floating around the academic world for decades are only the necessary but insufficient clues to the political psychology of the city. Obviously, the anonymity and atomization in a city are doubly seductive in a society scarred by socio-economic schisms and cultural hierarchies. A Dalit, landless, agricultural worker or a rural artisan seeking escape from the daily grind and violence of a caste society has reasons to value the impersonal melting pot of a metropolitan city. He is ever willing to defy the pastoralist's or the environmentalist's negative vision of the city. Because to lose oneself in the city is to widen one's freedom in a way not possible by migrating to another village, however distant from home. The colonial city made a place for itself in the Indian's fantasy life by promising that freedom in place of caste-specific vocations, ascribed status, and the crosscutting obligations of the *jajmani* system.

Less accessible to public awareness is the way many Indians have come to own up the colonial city as the self, the village as the other. The addictive charm of cities like Calcutta and Bombay lies in this play of the self. The village-as-the-other allows itself to be studied, measured, corrected, engineered. For even at its best, the village is uncivil by virtue of being closer to nature and the natural. At its worst, the village is a symbol of India's fearsome diversity and un-knowability. Colonial ethnography in Asia and Africa has turned the village into a summation of the feared, untamed fragments of one's self, scattered carelessly across a strange landscape.

This re-imagined village cannot take care of itself; it is the subaltern that cannot speak. All initiatives in the village, including remedies for social discrimination and institutionalized violence, must originate in the city. They can only be executed in the village. This presumption informs not merely the standard models of development, but even the revolutionary rhetoric concocted for the sake of the oppressed—by superbly read, well-motivated, urbane radicals, selflessly trying to occupy the moral high ground on behalf of the larger forces of history. The colonial city is now us, the non-village. It is now the new self, identified with history, progress, becoming.

As the flip side of the same story, the village of the imagination has become a serene, pastoral paradise. It has become the depository of traditional wisdom and spirituality, and of the harmony of nature, intact community life and environmental sagacity—perhaps even a statement of Gandhian austerity, limits to want, and anti-consumerism. The village, too, is no longer a village in itself; it is a counterpoint to the city. India lives in its villages—social reformers and political activists love to say, usually as a glib, ideological ploy. That statement has acquired a deeper meaning today. The village symbolizes control over self; the city reeks of self-indulgence and the absence of self-restraint. Beyond the temptations and glitter of the city lies the utopia of an idyllic, integrated, defragmented self, not tyrannized by the demands of atomized individualism. It is the utopia of the village as a self, controlling the self-that-is-the-city. The fear of the absence of self-restraint is actually the suspicion that one's control over one's self might have already partly collapsed.

The two co-ordinates—the infantilized village and the village as a geriatric responsibility—are not orthogonal, either in everyday life or in social theory. The former is the axis of the permissible way of looking at the world. The latter is the permissible way of dissenting, a luxury that those who can retreat from it into the 'realistic' world of a sweltering urban hothouse can sometimes afford.

As this image of the village encroaches upon larger areas of public awareness, it also begins to control the language of public life. Even those who do not live with such polarized images of the village and the city begin to use them as co-ordinates of their political idiom. Many public figures know that without invoking the first image of the infantilized village, waiting to pass its developmental milestones, they cannot hope to make sense even in their rural constituencies, where three-fourth of all Indians still live. But they also know that to participate now in national politics and pass the tacit censorship of the modern media, they have to make sense to the remaining one-fourth too. Hence, sometimes the strange spectacle of rural politicians in a predominantly rural society speaking of rural India as *if* they were from the cities. There is no escape from travelling to the village from the city any more. Arguably, this is the most important cultural change that has taken place in the region in recent decades.

Hence also the great contradictions associated with the imagination of the city in South Asia. Gandhi's savage critique of the railways as an agent of colonialism and his simultaneous use of railway journeys as a form of creative politics is only one such contradiction that centres around the idea of the journey. Likewise, the Naxalites, as committed Maoists, began with a theory of surrounding and defeating the city as the symbol of impersonal, institutionalized exploitation and immorality, but quickly converted their movement into a journey of self-discovery from the city to the village. The mix of idealism, innocence and sadomasochism in the movement made the rediscovery of the village and the global commons only a cover for the anguish of the urban, middle-class, upper-caste youth facing dispossession, meaninglessness and inner exile. Even the Dalits have increasingly brought to the city what is primarily a movement to restore justice and equity in the village.[10] Such contradictions are the very stuff of myths and they have helped make the myth of the journey to and from the city an organizing principle of the contemporary culture of Indian politics.

II

THE DECLINE IN THE IMAGINATION
OF THE VILLAGE

The obverse of the entry of the city as the locus of Indian consciousness is an erosion of the ability to imagine the village. By this I mean creative imagining—of the kind that invokes the fantasy of the 'archetypal', 'remembered' but nevertheless living Indian village—in those staying in villages and in others who have little or no connection with rural India. The erosion is not total; there *are* individuals whose works disprove the thesis of a decline. But, as a collectivity, creative Indians now have poorer access to the village of the imagination and the bonding that it once forged between individual creativity and its wider reception. The rest of this section spells out this proposition.

[10] Daya Pawar puts it movingly from the point of view of the Dalit youth when he speaks of Bombay in his autobiography: 'They say that Krishna tore Jarasandha in two pieces and threw them in opposite directions. In the same way in this city we are torn in two opposite directions. As I seek a place to merely rest my heart at the end of a hard day, all I have to come back to is a wretched hell that this city can offer.' Quoted in Vidyut Bhagwat, 'Bombay in Dalit Literature', Sujata Patel and Alice Thorner (eds), *Bombay: Mosaic of Culture* (Bombay: Oxford University Press, 1996), pp. 113–25; see p. 114. Bhagwat goes on to add, 'For the Dalit in the city, the new situation takes a tragic form. His flight from the culture of feudalism and face-to-face repression in the village offers him both the reality as well as the illusion of becoming a member of a free universe. But he soon realises that once again he remains an unnoticed, expendable stone at the base of the edifice of modernity. . . .', p. 115.

I begin with Mohandas Karamchand Gandhi (1861–1948), who is for many the ultimate exponent of the cultural principles enshrined in the Indian village. Gandhi took India's freedom movement to the village. He thought of the village as the basic unit of Indian civilization; and he envisioned the future of India around that of the village. Today, all major criticisms of village life as an anachronism, and the village as a change-resisting depot of popular superstitions, have as their locus a fear of Gandhi's vision of the future of India. It is the fear of a future that might be shaped in an open society by those whose minds we can no longer read.

Yet few know that the first time Gandhi came into direct, real-life contact with villages was when he reworked his political framework in his middle years. He was born in an urban family at Porbandar, a western Indian city, and was the son of a *dewan* or chief minister of a small princely state. He had his education in a city, at the ultra-élite Rajkumar College of Rajkot, and qualified for the Bar at London. He then worked in South Africa, where also he lived in cities, mainly at Durban. On his return to India he began to operate from the cities. It was only on the advice of his proclaimed guru Gopalkrishna Gokhale, the well-known public figure and freedom fighter, that Gandhi began to seriously explore rural India. That was in his late forties. The impact of the experience on him was deep, as though philosophically he had been preparing himself for it for years. After a while, it began to look as if he came from a village, as though he had lived in and fought for villages all his life.

How did a finished product of the city begin to speak and even look like a villager? Was there latent in Gandhi a retrievable imagination of the village which he could revive when he physically encountered the village? The answer may well be that the village was never dead within him. Its survival within him was ensured through the rituals, folklore, epics, legends and myths to which he was exposed through the traditions of his family, peer-group, caste, sect and language. That imagination was waiting to be reclaimed. When Gandhi reclaimed the village within him, he could easily slip into the role of a larger-than-life Indian village headman. He had been only apparently an outsider.[11]

If Gandhi's village is Indian public life's first village, Satyajit Ray's village is the cinema's first Indian village. Ray's debut film, *Pather Panchali*, many claim, is the greatest film ever made on village India. More than one critic has claimed that, for the world of cinema today, the Indian village is Ray's village.

Surprisingly, Ray's first genuine encounter with a village took place when he started shooting *Pather Panchali*: 'Until then I had no direct experience of what one meant when using the expression village life . . . we slowly developed an idea of the life described in the novel . . . Consequently, I had to depend on the descriptions in the original novel. The book, however, was an encyclopaedia of village life. However, I also knew that I could not depend only on it; that there were many things that I would have to discover myself.'[12]

Ray was born in a distinguished family settled in Calcutta for at least three generations. The family *did* have an estate in East Bengal (now Bangladesh) but, by the time he grew up, they had no access to that land. One gets a flavour of his family environment from some of its contributions to Bengal's social and cultural life: one of Ray's uncles introduced cricket in Bengal, another introduced detective fiction in Bengali literature by translating the Sherlock

[11] This retrievable imagination of the village is not the same as the timeless, fully autonomous, idyllic village that some social scientists constructed, following European travellers, colonial administrators and missionaries. See Ronald Inden, *Imagining India* (Oxford: Basil Blackwell, 1990).

[12] Satyajit Ray, *Apur Panchali* (Calcutta: Ananda, 1995), pp. 68–9.

Holmes stories. Ray's father, Sukumar Ray, arguably Bengal's most famous children's writer, ran a printing press and published a well-known magazine for children. It was a family known for its urbane cosmopolitanism and modern accomplishments. Naturally Ray was, and saw himself as, urban. He also had his early education in a quasi-Edwardian, élite public school, from within the walls of which the Indian village must have looked very distant indeed. The closest he came to a personal encounter with a village was when he sometimes visited villages during his student days at Visva-Bharati in Shantiniketan. Ray's relationship with the lifestyle of ordinary Bengalis can be gauged from his life-long practice of eating Bengali food with fork and knife, even the staple of rice and fish curry. In his early life, despite being partly educated in Shantiniketan, Ray had not heard much Indian music except Rabindrasangeet. He was brought up primarily on a diet of western classical music. Though he had studied Bengali as part of his course work, he had no self-confidence in handling the language. Upon graduation, when he took up a job in an advertisement agency, the firm was naturally British.

It was then that publisher Dilip Gupta of Signet Press invited Ray to illustrate an abridged, children's version of Bibhutibhushan Bandopadhyay's famous Bengali novel, *Pather Panchali*. The writer Sunil Gangopadhyay recounts how Gupta, shocked by the unsure Bengali of Sukumar Ray's son, gifted him Tarashankar Bandopa-dhyay's novel, *Kavi*.[13] Whether Ray read *Kavi* or not, his work for the illustrated version of *Pather Panchali*, published under the title *Aam Antir Bhepu*, changed his life. The book sparked his interest in Bengali literature and alerted him to the cinematic possibilities of *Panther Panchali*. Gangopadhyay adds that, if one compares the film script with the original novel, one finds that Ray's *Pather Panchali* is actually the children's version of the novel.

[13] Sunil Gangopadhyay, 'Priya Lekhak Satyajit Ray', in Shyamalkanti Das (ed.), *Lekhak Satyajit Ray* (Calcutta: Shivrani, 1993), pp. 17–20.

Where did Satyajit Ray, then, get his village? Why did his imagination of the village captivate his contemporaries, given his shallow acquaintance with it? Did the details of village life in the original novel ensure the authenticity of *Panther Panchali*, as Ray claimed? Or was it the poor exposure to village life of his audience? Given that *Pather Panchali* moved even those who knew village life first-hand, in this case, too, one is pushed to surmise that the imagination of the village was not dead—either in Ray or in his audience. It was there within him and in his immediate environs and, once he dipped into it, he could dredge up its formidable riches.

The village of the mind shapes the city of the mind, too. The novelist R.K. Narayan locates most of his stories in a small, imaginary town called Malgudi. By now, all English-speaking Indians and large parts of the Anglophone world know the town and its human-scale adventures and rhythm of life. By now, Malgudi is English literature's first Indian small town. It is such a living reality that one is sometimes surprised that maps do not show it; it is more real than many real-life Indian towns. Like Sherlock Holmes's Baker Street home in London, Malgudi deserves at least a gazetteer and a street directory.

The Malgudi stories supply clues to the imagery of the village that empowers the creativity of Gandhi and Ray. For, in these stories about a town, the village is a constant shadowy intruder. The village shapes the author's narrative of the town. Things happening at Malgudi cannot happen and characters at Malgudi cannot be what they are unless one imagines the surrounding villages telescoped into the town; many life stories in the town, in turn, branch out into these villages. These looming, omnipresent villages and the loveable absurdities their encroachment produces—defying a sophisticated, urbane author who lives in a city and has, therefore, chosen to write about urban life—give the Malgudi stories that lively, ambivalent link with their author and their wit and irony. The imagination of the village even links one to the city differently. For a city can also be mirrored in its antonym.[14]

Perhaps the cultural logic of an Indian city demands the presence of the village. Not merely sleepy Malgudi, but some of the more anguished metropolitan slums in literature, too, are infected or infiltrated by the village. As a result, the slum is left forever trying to re-invoke a remembered village under different guises. Sometimes this happens through the selective settlement of people (so that the slum becomes a ghetto of migrants from one particular caste, region, or language group) or through the way the slum mobilizes collective passions to configure its community life in an atomizing, steam-rolling metropolis (as in a primordial riot). Even Bombay commercial cinema and TV serials, so dependent upon the appeal of deliberately unrealistic, glamorized slums, invoke unashamedly the village community.[15] The imagery of the slum in a serial like Saeed Mirza's *Nukkad* is a key to its romance. What looks like a slum turns out to be, on closer scrutiny, a village that has survived the seductive glitter of the city. As an escape from the oppressive village, the slum captures, within the heartlessness of the city, the reinvented 'compassionate' village.[16]

---

[14] The reverse also is true; the village also can be defined by its antonym. Many environmental and alternative technology movements in India work with concepts of the village that bear an inverse relationship with the urban–industrial pathologies to which the Indian city is heir.

[15] Cf. R.A. Obudho and G.O. Aduwo, 'The Rural Bias of Kenya's Urbanisation', in J.B. Ojwang and J.N.K. Mugambi (eds), *The S.M. Otieno Case: Death and Burial in Modern Kenya* (Nairobi: Nairobi University Press, 1989), pp. 65–75.

[16] Ashis Nandy, 'Introduction: The Popular Cinema as the Slum's Eye View of Indian Politics', in Ashis Nandy (ed.), *The Secret Politics of Our Desires: Innocence, Culpability and Popular Cinema* (London: Zed Books and Delhi: Oxford University Press, 1998), pp. 1–18.

If Gandhi's village is the first Indian village of politics and Ray's that of the cinema, M.N. Srinivas' is the first Indian village of the social sciences. His famous texts have shaped the sociological imagination of the village for at least two generations of social scientists. In what U.R. Anantha Murthy calls Srinivas' greatest work, *The Remembered Village*, the author for once archly reveals the nature of his own emotional bonds with the village. Anantha Murthy's choice will not make sense to many academics, perhaps not even to Srinivas. For *The Remembered Village*, by the canons of the social sciences, is marred by tragic, empirical imperfections. Srinivas' data were burnt by mistake by an over-enthusiastic pack of radicals at a California think tank. Most social scientists consider the book scarred by that tragedy.

Anantha Murthy however is a writer, more at peace with human subjectivity. He cannot but admit the power of the imagery *The Remembered Village* invokes. Put heartlessly, to him Srinivas might have even been fortunate that his data got burnt and left him with only his memories. Surprisingly, some ethnographers seem to agree with Anantha Murthy.

What is important is . . . that most . . . think that Srinivas has succeeded in evoking the totality of village life in his account of it, that he has been able to vividly capture the human element and convey the 'feel' of Rampura to the reader. This is in contrast to his earlier major works in which we encounter no human beings, only customs and rules of social intercourse, only status structures and role occupants. . . . Chie Nakane suggestively compares *The Remembered Village* to a high-quality painting which, she writes, reveals more of the essence of a scene than does a photograph, by dramatising certain elements in it. Sol Tax's tribute to *Remembered Village* . . . as an ethnographic work which is also a work of art is echoed by most of the reviewers.

. . . Some readers will, perhaps, say that *Remembered Village* belongs more with the novels of Srinivas's famous friend, R.K. Narayan. It has the same emphasis on character and on the scenic in everyday life, the same delectable sense of humour as in Narayan's well-loved novels and stories about life in Malgudi. And did not Srinivas tell us in his *Social*

Change in Modern India that the sociologist who chooses to study his own society is rather like the novelist?[17]

Are these remarks an admission that Srinivas, by crossing the barriers between literature and the social sciences, has only enriched the latter? Or are they a homage to the creativity that, when forcibly distanced from hard empiricism, reaches paradoxically a higher order of empiricism?

This is the imagination of the village that has become a casualty of our times. The late Girilal Jain, for many years Editor of *The Times of India*, used to grumble, 'I don't want to go back to a village. Keep your Gandhi to yourself. You are from a city; you can speak for the village. I was brought up in a village. . . . My ideal India doesn't have a single village.' In that abhorrence, the village still had a place as a dystopia. On the other hand Sam Pitroda— for some years an icon and a mascot of modern, scientized India— is also from a village, belongs to an artisan caste, and once had close links with rural life. Indeed, he first used a telephone when he was twenty-one. Yet in his calculation of a future India there is neither hate nor love for the village. The village does not exist emotionally for him any more; he has cauterized it out of his self. In his algorithm of a creative society, villages are only statistics. One can do something for or to a village; a village cannot do anything for one or even itself.[18]

For a new generation of Indians, the village has increasingly become a demographic or statistical datum. Indian economists calculate national income and rural India's contribution to it; Indian sociologists and demographers know all about urban–rural

[17] T.N. Madan, *Pathways: Approaches to the Study of Society in India* (New Delhi: Oxford University Press, 1994), pp. 46, 48.

[18] Sam Pitroda, 'Development, Democracy, and the Village Telephone', *Harvard Business Review*, November–December 1993, pp. 66–79. This is in many ways a moving paper, which however also makes it absolutely clear the journey from the village to the city is for the likes of Pitroda, culturally and psychologically, a one-way journey.

differences in education, modern health care, and population growth. Policy-makers mark out 'backward areas' where new factories can be established or dams built as therapeutic measures. Entrepreneurs think of producing a village in the heart of Delhi, at Pragati Maidan or Hauz Khas, where the rich and the mighty may go and see rural India at weekends.[19] But the village is no longer a living presence in mainstream Indian intellectual life. In the various visions of the future floating around in the region there is much that is worthwhile, but not the vivacity of an imagined village. The village is quickly becoming a place where strangers live, where sati and untouchability are practised, where ethnic and religious riots have been taking place for centuries, and where, unless the civilized intervene, the inhabitants continue to pursue the sports of homicide and robbery.

Some may claim that that is another imagining of the village at play. But that imagining, unlike earlier ones, does not lead to any great creative effort. Nor does it resonate to the village of the mind in millions of others. Today, no film producer will finance a project like *Pather Panchali*—in this respect, nothing has changed since 1955 when Ray made his film—but, worse, no promising young filmmaker will choose to film something like *Pather Panchali* or, like Ray, pawn his wife's jewellery to do so. It is an open question whether that change has enriched or impoverished India's public culture.

One last word on the subject. Is the ability to reconnect to the shared village of the imagination only a matter of creative self-excavation? Or does it subsume the idea of mythic journey that

[19] Emma Tarlo, 'The Discovery and Recovery of "The Village" in Delhi: Hauz Khas 1986–94', Paper presented at the 13th European Conference of Modern Asian Studies in Toulouse, 31 August–3 September 1994.

some cannot but undertake, and others can but will not? True, during the last hundred years, the village *has* been for the urban Indian the destination of an epic journey of mind from which many have returned richer, deepened, and whole. But it is also true that, for others, the same journey has been a traumatic descent into a nether world of the self that corrodes physically and emotionally.[20] In either case, it becomes the obverse of the tragic journey from the village to the city that has been the standard marker of the hero in Indian popular literature and cinema.

India may live mainly in its villages, as the Gandhians insist, but it is no peasant society. Traditionally, the city has had a distinct and identifiable relationship with the village and that dyadic bond has been an important theme in classical plays, such as those of Bhasa, and in epics such as Mahabharata. This mutuality broke down with the entry of the colonial political economy in the nineteenth century, and since then the great Indian mythmakers have been trying to reconfigure it in new terms. Sometimes that reconfiguration has been sought in a civic life that recapitulates the village, sometimes in a village reconceived by the city. But the search has always been there—as an epic search for another vision of a desirable society and of a future that will not be entirely disjointed from the past.

III

THE REBIRTH OF THE HERO

The decline in the imagined village has altered the meaning of the journey between the village and the city in South Asia. It has become a journey from a disowned self to a self that cannot be fully owned up. The inner contradictions and tensions of the city-as-the-self, which trigger the painful journey back to the village,

---

[20] A brilliant 'take' on this journey is the short story by Premendra Mitra, 'Discovering Telenapota', Trs. Rina and Pritish Nandy, in Premendra Mitra, *Snake and Other Stories* (Calcutta: Seagull, 1990), pp. 1–10. We shall return to that journey in the third section of this book.

are often the exact reverse of the inner contradictions and tensions of the village, which triggered the fateful journey to the city in the first place. If the journey to the city was once an escape from oppressive sectarian and community ties, the demands of ascribed status, and the denial of individuality, the attempts to escape from the city are also often powered by dreams of an idyllic community and escape from hyper-competitive, atomized individualism.

The Indian city has re-emerged in public consciousness not as a new home, from within the boundaries of which one has the privilege of surveying the ruins of one's other abandoned homes. It has re-emerged as the location of a homelessness forever trying to reconcile non-communitarian individualism and associated forms of freedom with communitarian responsibilities, freely or involuntarily borne. Apparently, the city of the mind does not fear homelessness; it even celebrates homelessness. However, that merely camouflages the fear of a homelessness which can be cured only by a home outside home. Literature and serious cinema handle this issue as an inner conflict that defines a crisis of personal identity. Popular cinema sees it as a playful oscillation between the private and the public, the familial and neighbourly, the rustic and the urban.[21] The mother who is not the real mother but is more than one, the friend who becomes a brother and dies to prove the point, the self-destructive street urchin in love with a millionaire's daughter—in popular cinema, these are not merely anxiety-binding technologies of the self. They supply the cartography of a home away from home in a culture where homelessness, despair and the psychology of the outsider are all relatively new states of mind.

---

[21] See, for instance, the TV series by Ranjani Mazumdar and Shikha Jhingan, *The Power of the Image: The Tapori as Street Rebel* (New Delhi: BITV, 1998). Also, Ashis Nandy, 'An Intelligent Critic's Guide to Indian Cinema', *The Savage Freud and Other Essays in Possible and Retrievable Selves* (New Delhi: Oxford University Press, and Princeton, NJ: Princeton University Press, 1995), pp. 195–236; and 'Introduction: The Popular Cinema as the Slum's Eye View of Indian Politics'.

The slum and the street urchin defy the 'predatory identity' of the city—as Arjun Appadurai might identify the process—to paradoxically navigate the city more efficiently, perhaps even creatively.[22]

Serious Indian literature has never been comfortable with this oscillation. Such negotiation with the city has all the elements of the lowbrow and the maudlin and uses too narrow a range of psychological shades. But perhaps for that very reason, popular cinema has turned it into an over-used, proforma cliché.[23] Thus, the film persona of actor–director Raj Kapoor, one of those who presided over India's mythic world in the 1950s, was basically built around an ambivalent celebration of the city as street culture.[24] In *Awara* (1951) and *Shri 420* (1955), two immensely popular films that frame his work for most viewers, Kapoor is the ultimate street person, celebrating Bombay the way Woody Allen pays his reluctant, nervous homage to New York. Yet even in these films, the hero, while living by his wits off the street, turns the streets of Bombay into a friendly village neighbourhood. As a loveable cheat, pitted against more menacing well-bred sharks, Kapoor has moral and aesthetic unease with the city but, unlike Allen, that unease derives from outside the frame of civic values and the urban personality. Raj Kapoor's Bombay, like R.K. Narayan's Malgudi, is also a tribute to a remembered village.[25]

---

[22] For an elegant statement along these lines, see Mira Nair's *Salaam Bombay* (Bombay: 1988).

[23] For a more detailed discussion of the genre, see Ashis Nandy, 'The Popular Hindi Film: Ideology and First Principles', *India International Centre Quarterly*, 9(1), 1981.

[24] On the city as street culture, see the brief, suggestive essay by Arjun Appadurai, 'Street Culture', *India Magazine*, December 1987, 8, pp. 12–21.

[25] This also indirectly but powerfully emerges from Rajni Bakshi, 'Raj Kapoor: From *Jis Deshme Ganga Behti Hai* to *Ram Teri Ganga Maili*', in Ashis Nandy (ed.), *The Secret Politics of Our Desires: Innocence, Culpability and Popular Cinema* (London: Zed Books, and New Delhi: Oxford University Press,

The unease sharpens in what is arguably the only non-commercial film Kapoor produced, *Jagte Raho* (1956). Written and directed by Shambu Mitra and Amit Maitra, two theatre persons with no link with Bombay's commercial cinema, the film re-chronicles the tragicomic journey from the village to the city in *Shri 420* with a different ending. The hero of *Jagte Raho* never gets the chance to develop the street smartness of the earlier heroes to survive the ravages of everyday urban guerrilla warfare; he must depend more on his instincts for survival. This unequal battle makes the humour in *Jagte Raho* more bitter; it is mostly barbed sarcasm against the hypocrisy and corruption of the sophisticated urban rich. Indeed, the only time the hero feels at home in the city is when he finds himself among labourers in a slum, singing an evocative folk song identified with eastern Indian villages.

Jagte Raho is set in Calcutta. In it Kapoor, the heart-throb of millions, deglamorizes himself to play the role of a villager who, in search of drinking water, trespasses into a multistoreyed apartment building. There he witnesses the inner hollowness of civic life, while being pursued as a thief. At the end, when cornered, he confronts his pursuers and manages even to embarrass them. As he walks out of the heartless building, he finds at last a person—a young woman, played by the famous star Nargis in a one-scene appearance—willing to give him some water. Wearing the traditional Bengali sari, at the gate of an incongruous, old-style mansion with lush green trees, she gives water to the thirsty hero. The message is clearer in the Bengali version of the film, where the hero's dialect identifies him not only as a villager but as a refugee from East Bengal, a victim of the massive violence that accompanied the creation of independent India. He is in the city by default and

---

1998), pp. 92–133. The journey from the first to the second film in the title of Bakshi's paper can be read also as a perceived movement from the purity of the pastoral–civilizational values to the impurity of the urban–industrial values.

under duress. Home has to have a touch of the pastoral, even when a poisoned village has caused the homelessness. Home is 'natural' womanly nurture in a rediscovered village.

Few seem to love the city in its own terms in India, even among those who would prefer to lose their identity among its anonymous masses and seem eager to extol that loss.

The mythic frame within which these oscillations fit is best reflected in the character of Karna in the Mahabharata.[26] Though Karna as the hero of the Mahabharata was not entirely unknown in pre-modern times, during the last century the character has been a particularly sensitive index of changes in Indian definitions of the ideal self, mediating between the village and the city. The journey of Karna is a remarkable testimony to the way a living myth in an epic culture—as against myths in cultures that have epics—can act as an alternative record of the shifting psychological contours of a culture. Indeed, during the last two decades, I have had to return more than once to the trajectory of Karna's life to trace the course of India's ambivalent relationship with the urban–industrial vision.[27]

[26] In a fascinating paper, M.K. Raghavendra argues that there has been no new myth in Indian popular cinema, which by its own conventions must avoid a linear, historical narrative. As a result, such cinema cannot but be grounded in the myths of India's ancient epics. While there is an important element of truth here, one reason for the scarcity of new myths in Indian popular cinema could be the pliability and built-in diversity of the myths in Indian epics. They absorb, interpret, and reconfigure new experiences, particularly new anxieties and fantasies, within the old myths. The myths do not become linear or historically tinged thereby, but history and time acquire different meanings in cinema. M.K. Raghavendra, 'Time and the Popular Film', *Deep Focus*, 1992, 4(1), pp. 10–18.

[27] Ashis Nandy, *Alternative Sciences: Creativity and Authenticity in Two Indian Scientists*, 2nd edition (New Delhi: Oxford University Press, 1995), Part I; and 'An Intelligent Critic's Guide to Indian Cinema'.

It is true that at least one other character in the Mahabharata has sometimes been an index of the cultural status of the journey to the modern city—namely Krishna. Numerous influential re-interpretations of Krishna's life and teachings during the last hundred years bear witness to this. However, Krishna is less relevant to our story because his break with his pastoral past is complete in most Mahabharatas and even the memory of that past does not play any role in his life as a king in an imperial city. Karna, though entirely urban, is dogged by his ambivalence towards the city; it does not often look to him adequately civic. The journey to the city is never complete for him. Naturally, he has served as a projective test for Indians caught in the same ambivalence towards the village, as a home and as a prototype of Indian civilization.

Both Sigmund Freud and Ernest Jones have identified Karna as a classic hero, part of a long series beginning from antiquity and including Sargon, Moses, Oedipus, Cyrus, Perseus, Romulus, Paris and Heracles.[28] At least three elements in Karna's life conform to the paradigmatic life of the hero, according to Freud and Otto Rank: his mysterious birth, his first journey through water in a basket, and his humble foster parents who do not know the secret of his divine and royal origins.[29] There are also similarities between Karna and Freud's Moses who, unlike the Biblical Moses, is a scion of the Egyptian aristocracy and leads the enslaved Israelis to freedom, in a mythic unfolding of the oedipal drama. In Karna's case, the situation is reversed; he fights his own brothers, not knowing who he really is. However, it is an indicator of the

---

[28] Sigmund Freud, *Moses and Monotheism*, trs. Katherine Jones (London: Hogarth, 1940), p. 17.

[29] Ibid., Otto Rank, *The Myth of the Birth of the Hero*, trs. Philip Freund (New York: Alfred Knopf, 1959). Karna was born through his mother's ear. For a classical psychoanalytic study of the rich meanings associated with birth through the ear, see Ernest Jones, 'The Madonna's Conception through the Ear: A Contribution to the Relation between Aesthetics and Religion', *Psycho-Myth, Psycho-History: Essays in Applied Psychoanalysis* (New York: Hillstone, 1974).

vibrant presence of the mythic in India that whereas Freud's Moses is a marginal presence in contemporary Jewish consciousness, the various modern incarnations of Karna have carved out a place for themselves in contemporary India. Indeed, the traditional and modern Karnas coexist in reasonable amity in the Indian imaginary.

Karna might meet the classical criteria of the hero the world over, but he has won wide acceptability in India as the hero of Mahabharata only during the last hundred years. In the better known and more popular Mahabharatas, Krishna, Arjuna, Yudhisthira and, less frequently, Bhima have contested for that status. All these contestants have less-well-kept secrets of birth that should qualify them as heroes in textbooks of psychoanalysis. The new preference for Karna cannot be explained away as only a 'natural' cultural move towards the universal model for a mythic hero.

Karna's journey in Vyasa's Mahabharata begins with his natural mother Kunti, a princess, getting a boon that allows her to have a child by any god she wishes, provided she goes through a specific set of prayers/rituals. She first invokes, while still unmarried, the sun god. But when, as a result, she conceives and gives birth to a son, she fears a scandal and stealthily puts the child in an ornate casket and floats it on the Ashva river, from where it finally floats down the more sacred Jamuna and Ganga. A humble, childless charioteer, Adhiratha, and his wife, Radha, discover the baby. They bring him up as their son. Kunti later marries Pandu, the sickly prince of Hastinapur. A sage has cursed Pandu to die if sexually aroused. So he allows his two wives to use Kunti's boon to have children by the gods. As a result, the two queens become the mothers of five sons, the Pandavas. When Madri commits suicide after the death of Pandu, Kunti becomes the guardian of all five. Pandu's blind brother Dhritarashtra, father of a hundred sons known as the Kauravas, becomes the new king of Hastinapur.

Karna grows up to become a gifted warrior, known for his bravery, self-destructive generosity and truthfulness. However, he also has other qualities that make him the most controversial character of the Mahabharata. These are revealed as he journeys through his life. From his early years he is subjected to the barbs and contempt of many as a lowborn nurturing inappropriate princely ambitions. He is particularly sensitive to such jibes. His first serious encounter with the Pandavas, the five legitimate children of Kunti, takes place in his youth. Once, when the Pandavas and the Kauravas are being trained in armed conflict by their guru, Karna impulsively challenges them to compete with him. Neither the guru nor his disciples pick up the challenge; competing with princes is also a princely privilege. As it happens, Karna has already befriended Duryodhana, the eldest among the Kauravas, who see the Pandavas as rivals. Duryodhana now shrewdly makes Karna the king of Anga. But birth still stands in Karna's way. His foster father, Adhiratha, comes to bless him before the competition and this reveals his humble origins. Karna is ridiculed and driven away.

Karna's next encounter with the Pandavas ends in even greater bitterness. Princess Draupadi decides to marry the winner in an archery competition. Karna wants to compete; so does Kunti's third son Arjuna, sired by Indra, king of the gods. Once again Karna is humiliated; Draupadi refuses to marry a charioteer's son even if he wins. Karna now turns even more hostile to the Pandavas and becomes even more defensively loyal to Duryodhana.

The Kauravas try to dispossess the Pandavas of their share of the kingdom in various ways. After defeating the Pandavas in a dishonest game of dice, they exile the Pandavas from Hastinapur for thirteen years. When the Pandavas return from their exile, Duryodhana again refuses to share the kingdom with them. The

doting father, Dhritarashtra, fails to check his sons. A battle becomes inevitable.

Karna naturally decides to fight for the Kauravas. However, on
the eve of the battle, Lord Krishna goes to Karna's camp, reveals
to him the secret of his birth, and requests him to fight for the
Pandavas. He offers Karna, technically the eldest Pandava, the
kingdom of Hastinapur in the event of victory, the unconditional
loyalty of his five younger brothers, and the hand of Draupadi in
marriage. (Though Arjuna had won the archery competition and
the right to wed Draupadi, due to a careless comment by Kunti
she is now married to all the five Pandavas.) Karna turns down the
offer. He says that even if he is made king of Hastinapur, he will
have to give away the kingdom to Duryodhana and that would not
be fair to Yudhisthira. Kunti now goes to meet Karna and asks for-
giveness for abandoning him. She begs him to change sides and
spare the lives of her children. At this point even the sun god ap-
pears and tells Karna to obey his mother for his own good. However, Karna is already an orphan psychologically; he refuses to
betray a loyal friend who had made him a king and a kshatriya,
a status his own mother denied him. However, Karna promises
not to touch any of his brothers except Arjuna. He consoles Kunti
that, at the end of the war, she will have her five sons intact, with
or without Karna. In the war the inevitable happens. Karna dies
battling Arjuna. However, Arjuna has to flout the codes of warfare at the instigation of Krishna, serving as his charioteer, to kill
Karna. Only then do the Pandavas come to know Karna's true
identity and sadly and guiltily perform his last rites.

Exactly, a hundred years ago, in 1898, the famous physicist turned
plant physiologist Jagadis Chandra Bose (1858–1937), already a

living legend, wrote a letter to his friend, the famous poet Rabindranath Tagore (1861–1941). Bose was the first scientist in India who self-consciously tried to pattern a culturally rooted identity for Indian scientists and, when he wrote to Tagore, Tagore was already a public figure from a family that had played a leading role in the modernization of India. In his letter Bose pleaded with his friend to write on the life and the fate of Karna. Bose felt that Karna was the real hero of the Mahabharata and deserved revaluation.

Of uncertain birth, insecure, defiant, and unwilling to adjust to his ascribed status as the son of a humble charioteer, Karna seemed to symbolize the predicament of the self-made person in a society not fully receptive to individualism and competitiveness. Bose wanted Tagore to grant Karna the justice that was denied him in life. Tagore accepted the challenge and wrote a verse play, *Karna-Kunti-Samvad*, a reconstruction of Karna's last encounter with his mother Kunti.[30] The play captures the anguish behind Karna's free-floating violence and arrogance and his response to his illegitimate birth and the trauma of maternal rejection. In the play Karna knows he is on the losing side but tells his mother that he cannot, on those grounds, abandon the losing side. Karna's death in the battle of Kurukshetra has thus an element of self-destruction. He can escape his fate but refuses.

The rivalry between Karna and Arjuna has many layers. A pantheistic world reflects the eternal, natural conflict and rivalry between Indra, the king of the gods, whose personal weapon is thunder, and Surya, the sun god. On this plane the battle between Karna and Arjuna is a clash between two cosmic forces. At another plane, Karna's is an infinitely sad story of a person fighting a society insensitive to his desperate attempts to break out of ascribed status, to seek sanction for competitive individualism and personal

---

[30] Rabindranath Tagore, 'Karna-Kunti Samvad', *Rachanavali* (Calcutta: Government of West Bengal, 1999), vol. 3, pp. 145–50.

achievement, and his rage at the failure to do so.[31] It is the story of a charioteer's son who becomes a great warrior, keeps the company of kings, and hankers for upper-caste status, not knowing that by birth he has a right to that status. Bitterness pushes him to the margins of ethics. Bose identifies with Karna's anguish. His plea to the most respected Indian writer of his generation is a plea to legitimize the first modern Indian in India's epic culture. Seeking acceptance for Karna must have meant for Bose seeking acceptance for his values.

In the hundred years since Bose wrote his letter, Karna has reappeared on and off to haunt India's urban middle class. Attempts to reinterpret him as a wronged hero, victimized by an unjust society, obdurately hostile to the norms of equity, have recurred. Novels like Shivaji Sawant's *Mrityunjaya* and plays like Buddhadev Bose's *Prathama Partha* have contributed to the effort. In theatre, Karna's chequered career during the last hundred years has ended with Peter Brooke's Mahabharata, in which he is the hero. In cinema, Shyam Benegal's *Kalyug* locates Karna in the ruthless world of corporate rivalry, facing an unjust fate, a meaningless clan war, and conventional morality.[32] In all these incarnations, Karna is explicitly a double of Arjuna, whom Karna partly dislodges as the hero of Mahabharata.

Popular culture has returned to the myth less selfconsciously but with more vigour. Kunti, Karna, and Arjuna cast their shadows on a number of characters and plots in the commercial cinema. One of the better-known efforts in the genre, *Deewar* (1974), is identified in public memory with the emergence of a hero whom some critics have described as the first urban–industrial man in Indian popular cinema. In this film the rivalry between two brothers takes many forms but finally centres on recognition and

---

[31] Ashis Nandy, *Alternative Sciences: Creativity and Authenticity in Two Indian Scientists* (New Delhi: Oxford University Press, 1995).

[32] Nandy, 'An Intelligent Critic's Guide to Indian Cinema'.

acceptance by their mother. In this now-stereotyped story of two brothers who take to the city in different ways, one grows up to become a police officer, the other a criminal. The criminality is shown to be a response to injustice and feelings of rejection; the anger against an unjust society finds voice in asocial violence. The police officer acts like the hand of destiny, backed by the mother's moral convictions and her identification with him. When, at the end, the police officer shoots his brother in the course of his duty, the hero dies in his mother's arms, completing the tragic journey of a wronged, discarded child who grows up to become a street-smart, urban warrior, negotiating life mainly through the technology of violence. *Deewar*'s hero is the prototypical urban man, but somewhere along the way he has fought for and lost his mother's acceptance. That acceptance comes posthumously and hardly absolves the modern metropolis of its moral culpability.

Mani Ratnam's *Dal-pati* (1994), which retells the story of Karna, never seriously deviates from the conventions of popular cinema and the stylization that goes with them. However, it anticipates the director's later films, especially, the taut, thriller-like narrative he weaves around an epic journey to a strange city that becomes a nightmare and yet, at the same time, expands and enriches the self. In all, 'enemies' turn out to be bound by deeper ties to the self and women mediate between apparently incompatible psychological worlds through a form of maternity that deepens conjugality. All are recurrent themes in popular creative imagination and no amount of erudite film criticism is likely to dent Mani Ratnam's popularity or wean him off the cocktail of the classical, the folk, and the slum-tinged urbanity in which he specializes.[33]

Dal-pati begins in an idyllic village where a teenaged mother delivers an illegitimate son. The next scene shows the mother sobbing and running after a goods train speeding towards the city; she

---

[33] Nandy, 'Introduction: The Popular Cinema as the Slum's Eye View of Indian Politics'.

has abandoned her child in a pack of hay in the train. As in most popular films in India, the journey takes a dramatic, if predictable, course—the pack falls from the train while it is crossing a bridge and the child floats down the river to a town where a poor, low-caste woman picks him up and names him Suraj (the Sun). The motif of the train, whistling through dark tunnels while rushing towards the city, the journey over a river in a basket of hay, and the discovery of the child by a poor Shudra woman—these are all perfectly congruent with the themes Freud and Rank consider pivotal to the life of a mythic hero. Only, the fantasies centring on the birth of the hero get intertwined in this instance with themes of a humbler but anguished, angry rebirth. The child grows up to become the warlord of an urban slum. He knows his own past and is sensitive about his status as a person of unknown origins; the history of maternal rejection haunts him at every moment. His violence and rejection of social norms are shown to be natural products of his personal history.

We next see Devraj, a local don, befriending Suraj and appointing him the *dal-pati* or leader of his gang, even though Suraj has killed one of the gang. The friendship with Devraj earns Suraj the enmity of a criminal politician from whom Devraj has broken away.

The mystery of his birth continues to hound Suraj. When he falls in love, Devraj tries to arrange a marriage with the consent of the girl's father. The father refuses to marry his daughter to a person of unknown birth. At this point a commissioner, Arjuna, is posted in the city. He is accompanied by his parents. Soft-spoken and urbane, firm and incorruptible, Arjuna is keen to establish the authority of law. However, he meets little success. People come to respect him as honest and well-meaning but remain loyal to Devraj and Suraj and the alternative, street-based, justice system they have founded. To complicate matters, Arjuna's mother spots Suraj's former girlfriend, comes to like her, and arranges her marriage with Arjuna.

Regular viewers of Indian popular cinema will not be surprised that, through the course of events, Arjuna's father finds out that his wife is also the mother of the disreputable, violence-prone prince of the slum. In an epic culture, predictability is an inalienable part of popular drama and the director has already strewn plenty of clues about the story he is telling. The father now goes to meet Suraj to request him to give up Devraj and rejoin the family. Suraj refuses, vowing that he will 'live and die with Devraj', but promises to spare Arjuna. Suraj also begs his father not to reveal his identity to his mother. 'I was a scandal for her; the one who has reared me is my real mother', he says. To keep his promise he now goes to the officer's bungalow and, to Arjuna's amazement, requests him to leave the city. At this point, once again predictably, chaotic violence breaks out: the rival gang of the politician Devraj has ditched shoots Devraj, and Suraj kills the politician. However, his mother also comes to know the truth at last. She has pined for her lost child all her life; the discovery of Suraj and the divide between him and the family nearly leads to her breakdown. But she recovers her wits quickly enough to have an emotional reunion with her lost child.

Dal-pati is arguably the final, triumphant incarnation of Karna for our times. He is no longer a tragic figure who wins mythic immortality by defying fate, almost as a compensation for what he misses out in life. This time even his mother goes to live with him, in preference to Arjuna, presumably to expiate for the past.[34] Karna has won his final battle.

The associations which the personality of Karna has picked up since the late nineteenth century are not simple variations on the

---

[34] Is the myth itself undergoing some long-term changes, in response to changes in public consciousness? *Dal-pati* has been followed by another, even more mediocre film, *Karan Arjun*, in which a wronged mother unleashes against her oppressors—led by the bad father, an exploitative village landlord—her two sons, Karna and Arjuna. They are no longer rivals but mutually complementary instruments of their mother's wrath.

age-old myth of the hero. Karna and Arjuna have become two faces of modern urbanity. The total acceptance of Karna by his mother in *Dal-pati* suggests that they might have become, more directly, each other's double. Mani Ratnam could have, following popular cinematic conventions, used the same actor to play both the roles. Perhaps the split between the village and city, and the movement from one to the other, are now acquiring other overtones.

Rajnikant, the popular star playing Suraj, is dark, direct, and speaks rustic Bhojpuri when young and the language of the Bombay slum when older. He seems a natural counterpoint to the chocolate-pie hero, Arvind Swamy who, as Arjun, is fair, urbane, speaks chaste Hindi, and is identifiably Brahminic. Arjuna looks and behaves like a son of his parents and the husband of his wife; Suraj looks and behaves like a misfit in polite society. The contrast hints at possibilities that Bose and Tagore might not have thought of in 1898.

Heisham Kanhailal's play *Karna* further develops the social overtones the epic hero is now acquiring. Using the classical Manipuri dance form as an integral, stylized medium of theatre, the play choreographs the identity of Karna into a prism and a projection of the inner tensions of modern cosmopolitanism in India. For the first time, the locus of tragedy is not in the personality of Karna or in the cosmic order—in the eternal, fated, natural hostility between Indra and Surya—but in the humiliation of his foster parents and the community that reared him in an unjust, unequal social order. The play begins with Karna's last battle and death at Kurukshetra. A perplexed, shocked Arjuna learns the secret of Karna's birth from a shrewd, somewhat wily Krishna and sees the body of Karna become a new battleground between those wanting to give Karna an 'appropriate' royal funeral and the low-caste community that had known him as a part of itself till then. Above all, the body becomes a battleground between a triumphant, arrogant, queenly Kunti, who has rejected Karna in life but wants to possess him in death, and his rustic, humble,

Shudra foster mother, Radha, lamenting the death of one who had lived and died as her son. In life, Karna might have spurned the kingdom of Hastinapur for the sake of his foster parents; in death, Kunti wins. In the lament of the Shudras, though, there is intimation of rebelliousness. Towards the end of the play a possessed Shudra woman in a frenzied, almost violent dance, signals resistance and a language of dissent not accessible to those who see the mystery of Karna's birth as the first marker of his self. The dance anticipates the violence that becomes overt in some of the popular cinematic versions of Karna's life.

Kanhailal's *Karna* is an exception, for it bypasses Karna's character as a clue to his tragedy. His Karna walks out of the pages of the Mahabharata to seek power and legitimacy for the rustic, the non-canonical and the lowborn in a secular city. Otherwise, not only are Karna's virtues fairly constant over his various literary or cinematic incarnations, but also his fatal flaws of character. Even those who have revalued his defiance of ascriptive status and his celebration of competitive achievement and fierce individualism have not much to say about his arrogance and narcissism. The recent readings have not changed Karna's traits, only their evaluation. They assume that the source of Karna's tragedy is not any fatal flaw of character, but the fatal flaw of a society unable to live with his tough, competitive individualism and drive for achievement.

However, there is an aspect of Karna that the older readings sense but cannot articulate, and the new readings—in awe of the once-devalued traits that now rule the world—cannot even acknowledge: Karna's failure to link his private battle against injustice and fate to any larger struggle for justice and mastery over fate. Only Kanhailal unwittingly recognizes this when he casts Karna in a just war *after* his death.

Perhaps the older readings of Karna are not as unjust as Bose had thought. They *do* read Karna, cramped by what Wilhelm Reich might have diagnosed as his fatal character armour, as incapable of extricating the record of his suffering from his personal interests or memories of personal slights.[35] It was as if Karna sought to establish a narcissistic monopoly on his experience of victimization and to turn it into a source of grudge against the world. No means, however low, are unacceptable to this otherwise majestic, generous person, to protect the self-indulgence that accompanies that monopoly. He shows no awareness that his suffering can become a shareable tragedy only when it transcends the specificity of a case and stands witness for all other victims of similar suffering. He cannot admit that a victim's experience acquires moral grandeur and a higher level of authenticity only when he or she is willing to represent the victimization of others caught in similar hinges of fate.[36]

Karna's final posthumous triumph, therefore—his journey from the city of the past to the city of the future, adorned by values associated with the urban–industrial vision—is unlikely to be a secure one. Handicapped by the absence of any basic trust in his social world, his identification with the arrogant, powerful king Duryodhana reflects not only fraternal loyalty but also a Faustian compact.

Yet, paradoxically, Karna's vision remains wider than Arjuna's, the victorious prince who fights on the side of virtue. Karna has seen life bottom upwards; he has seen the city as an outsider.

---

[35] For instance, this awareness implicitly colours Irawati Karve, 'Karna', *Yuganta: The End of an Epoch* (Bombay: Popular Prakashan, 1969), pp. 167–88. Though the concept of character armour is Reich's, a sensitive use of it in the case of a mythic character is in Ernest Becker, 'The Pawn Broker: A Study in Basic Psychology', *Angel in Armor: A Post-Freudian Perspective on the Nature of Man* (New York: Free Press, 1969), pp. 73–100.

[36] I am here speaking not merely of individuals but also of communities and cultures. In our times, the inability of the Israeli state and sections of the Israeli society and the North American Jewish diaspora to generalize the experience of the European holocaust of the 1940s, one of the greatest tragedies in recent centuries, is also a narcissistic failure. By a tragic turn of events, the Jewish holocaust is increasingly becoming for some parts of the world *only* a Jewish holocaust and less of a shared symbol for the millions of other victims of exterminatory machines of violence.

Arjuna, though forced to play humble roles (a dance teacher, for instance, during the great exile), has not. When Karna makes the devastating proposition to his mother—that she will have to be satisfied with five sons because she can either have Arjuna or him—it is only partly a homage to jealousy and hatred. For Karna does not totally disown his newly discovered relationships; he promises not to kill his other brothers. His knowledge of his self has expanded. Indeed, that knowledge cramps him as a warrior when he fights Arjuna at Kurukshetra. Arjuna does not know who Karna is; he has no sympathy for the lonely warrior, simultaneously battling his arch enemy, his brother, and his own self.

In his new incarnations, too, the journey of Karna is the journey of the wronged, discarded child who goes on to become a shrewd urban warrior negotiating life mainly through violence. The paradigmatic urban man, more at home in the metropolitan slum than in palaces or fields, hides behind his arrogance and certitudes his inner battles with the memory of a rejecting mother who stands for continuity, community and nature. The legitimacy of the city is incomplete, given that primordial rejection.

2

The City as the Invitation to an Antique Death

Pramathesh Chandra Barua and the Origins of the Terribly Effeminate, Maudlin, Self-destructive Heroes of Indian Cinema

The person who most dramatically symbolized the capacity of the new forms of popular culture to express some of the changing concerns of Indian society—concerns that could no longer be handled within the traditional, more enduring art forms—was actor–director Pramathesh Chandra Barua (1903–51). He may not have been the greatest among the early generation of film directors, but he was one of the larger-than-life figures that Indians learnt to associate with these new modes of self-expression. Barua represented, in the popular imagination, the final triumph of the worldview of Saratchandra Chattopadhyay (1876–1938) and the especial meaning the novelist gave to the journey from the village to the city and, sometimes, to the tragic, ill-fated, and desperate attempts to return to the village from the city. So authoritative was the presence of this mythic journey that all other modes of creativity had to define themselves in opposition to it, and, to that extent, had to remain captive to it.[1]

---

[1] One of the first serious attempts to examine the mythic stature of the journey between the village and the city, and the time travel involved in it, can

Thus, Satyajit Ray was dismissive about the films and director-ial skills of Barua, whom he saw as the most respected mascot of popular cinema in India and as the ultimate index of the state of public taste. Ray considered Barua's cinema stylized, unrealistic, imitative, dependent on heavy make-up and stilted dialogue. He believed he had learnt nothing from this part of his ancestry. In contrast, Ritwik Ghatak once said: 'To my mind P.C. Barua is the greatest director till date. I have heard modern-day directors have made very good use of "subjective camera". But they have a long way to go and could have learnt a lot from Barua.'[2]

Why this strange discrepancy in the evaluation of a filmmaker by the two greatest names in Indian art cinema? At first, the answer may seem obvious. Ray defined himself in defiance of and in op-position to the worldview Barua and Saratchandra consecrated, and so Ray's self-definition had to include an element of aggressive negation of Barua. Ghatak, on the other hand, belonged psycholo-gically to a generation that had seen the beginning of the decline of Saratchandra and Barua in the aesthetic sensitivities of the ur-ban middle class, for the break with Barua and Saratchandra in ci-nema had already been made by Ray. Indeed, Ghatak had also to deal with Ray, already identifiable as the authoritative voice of a new tradition in Indian cinema. Here, I shall give the same answer

---

be found in Chidananda Dasgupta's *The Painted Face: Studies in India's Popu-lar Cinema* (New Delhi: Roli Books, 1991), ch. 3.

[2] Ritwik Ghatak, 'Film' (1966), quoted in Debolina Barua, 'Pramathesh Barua', unpublished paper, 1994. See also Ritwik Ghatak, 'Bengali Cinema: Literary Influence', in *Cinema and I* (Calcutta: Ritwik Memorial Trust, 1987), pp. 21–5, 22–3: '. . . even in the olden days, there were some exceptions to formula film making. The name P.C. Barua comes to mind. Here was a man who, in the late thirties, sometimes explored the potentialities of this plastic medium. His *Grihadaha* marks some of the earliest successful and significant transitions in films. In his *Uttarayan*, he utilised the subjective camera to telling effect. Surrounded by mediocrity, he sometimes gave off sparks of pure cinema. Though, in the ultimate analysis, he remained a product of his milieu.'

in a roundabout fashion, in the hope that the attempt will also tell us something about the core fantasies and mythic life that Indian popular cinema copes with, particularly the changing poetics of the hero which links such cinema to its audience.

I

THE JOURNEY TO THE CITY

Pramathesh Barua was the first son of the ruler of a tiny native state, Gauripur, in eastern India. Though called a princely family, the Baruas were only the owners of a large estate. They were Kayasthas, and were connected with the better-known ruling family of Cooch Behar. Gauripur was at the margins of Bengal and Assam, geographically and culturally. It even had its own dialect, Gauripuri, which appeared to bridge Bengali and Assamese. This marginality—actually a form of biculturality—was reflected in the family culture of the Baruas. Despite the name Barua, usually an Assamese surname (though also found in East Bengal), the family was deeply immersed in Bengali traditions and Pramathesh himself wrote and sang elegantly in Bengali. His scripts and letters, though often unbearably maudlin and purple, are a testimony to his mastery over the Bengali language and it is said that the legendary singer Kundanlal Saigal, after listening to Barua sing some Bengali songs at a party, felt Barua was a better singer than he himself was.[3] Satyajit Ray's suggestion that Barua 'naturally' escaped overacting in his films because of his inadequate command over Bengali is obviously uncharitable and an attempt to rationalize his deeper discomfort with Barua.[4] Chidananda Dasgupta, the distinguished film critic and Ray's friend and biographer, is more perspicacious in this respect. While sharing some of Ray's antipathy

[3] Rabi Basu, 'Rajar Kumar', *Desh*, 1976, Vinodon No. (1383), pp. 194–235. This long essay, though marred by hyperbole, is an excellent source of information on Barua.

[4] Satyajit Ray, 'Atiter Bangla Chavi', *Vishaya Chalacchitra* (Calcutta: Ananda, 1982), 2nd edn., p. 40.

towards Barua, Dasgupta suggests that Barua deliberately opted for understatement and intelligent use of his voice.

Young Pramathesh was close to his mother, a devout Vaishnava in a Shakto household, and an excellent singer. It may be of some interest to the psychologically minded that, after being weaned, he lived entirely on milk for eight years. He had his first solid food at the age of nine when the customary ritual of *annaprashan* was celebrated. Whether as a consequence or not, he remained a Spartan eater all his life. His food habits were to pose a problem in his later life, when he contacted tuberculosis. There also persisted in Barua a strange but identifiable sense of exile from a maternal utopia, alongside attempts to regain it through fleeting relationships with women and through fantasies of lover–mothers at the margins of social morality (providing absolute, unconditional nurture as a substitute for lost love-objects). Later, these associations and imageries were to entwine with what many consider the central motif of his work, namely the sense of exile that came from his ambivalence towards the village and the city, and the journey from one to the other. Barua's relationship with his mother, though described by many as idyllic, probably had more to it than meets the eye. It is not insignificant that the two events involving his mother most— as friends and relatives recount—were both sources of acute frustration for the son: his arranged marriage, and his inability to go to England for higher studies. More about these later.

Throughout life Pramathesh admired his father Prabhatchandra, a learned man with an excellent knowledge of literature and classical music, a social reformer, a patron of education and music, and a builder. Prabhatchandra was fond and proud of his eldest son and heir, almost blindly so. He granted Pramathesh enormous freedom from an early age and, afterwards, though often shocked by his son's chaotic marital life and financial problems, Prabhatchandra continued to have faith in his unconventional but brilliant son. However, the father–son relationship had its underside. Pramathesh pushed his father's faith in him to the brink at every opportunity. At the same time, he followed up some of his major transgressions, the ones he knew would hurt his father, by writing self-abnegating, guilt-ridden letters to Prabhatchandra.

Though his parents had two other sons and two daughters, they doted on Pramathesh, their eldest son—with reason. Pramathesh was born to his parents after years of childlessness, reportedly after they received the blessings of a Himalayan sadhu. Another version of the story says the couple had a child eight years earlier, who died soon after birth; Pramathesh was born only after the sadhu intervened.

Pramathesh lost his mother when he was twenty-two, and this was a traumatic loss. His father lived till 1945 and saw his son acquire immense fame. But after the mid-1930s, he probably did not see much of his son, for Pramathesh's visits to Gauripur became infrequent after his scandalous second marriage.

Barua's early education began at home under a private tutor. As the scion of a princely family he learnt to fire a gun even before learning to read and write. By the time he was twelve he had already bagged his first tiger, at the time viewed as sure sign of a great sportsman. He played billiards superbly, tennis and badminton reasonably well. Later, he was to become an expert rider and, still later, owned a number of race horses.

From an early age, Barua fitted middle-class India's, especially Bengal's, idea of a romantic hero. Remarkably handsome, with a poetic and fragile look and a pronounced touch of the androgynous, his appearance and style were thrown into relief by his paradoxical fascination with big-game hunting and philandering. It seemed as if popular markers of the hero aroused anxieties about sexual identity in him, and he had to try to reaffirm his masculinity in other areas of life. Barua's life was a bundle of paradoxes in other ways too. His interest in hunting went with a lifelong distaste for meat, fish and eggs (which he had probably picked up from his Vaishnava mother) and his conspicuously pacifist, almost ascetic style. After bagging a large number of heads, in later life he gave up hunting.

When young, Pramathesh wanted to be a doctor—because he wanted to serve the people of his state, he later claimed. His father even modernized the local hospital at his behest. Later, he went to Calcutta's well-known Hare School and, for a while, to Shantini-ketan, when Rabindranath Tagore was still very active at the school. At the end of his schooling, at the age of fourteen, he was married to Madhurilata, the eleven-year-old daughter of one Birendranath Ganguly of Calcutta. It was an arranged marriage; the initiative in the matter was taken by his mother. Her precocious son was already in love with the daughter of a doctor at Dhubri but had to comply with his mother's wishes.

In 1918, at the age of fifteen, Barua joined Calcutta's Presidency College to study science. The college attracted the cream of eastern India's youth and its alumni were a conspicuous presence in India's public life. It was still one of India's premier experimental laboratories for testing out new ideas from the West. However, the city had a greater impact on young Pramathesh than his college. It helped him develop an active interest in theatre, and he organiz-ed a company in his native Gauripur to stage plays that had prov-ed successful in Calcutta's commercial theatre. His style of acting then bore the stamp of the famous actor Sisir Kumar Bhaduri. That was not all: Pramathesh also successfully played a number of female roles. Satyajit Ray's other proposition—that Barua, perhaps despite trying, could not overact or be stagy because he had no exposure to theatre—is therefore as unconvincing as his jibe at Barua's Bengali.[5]

In 1924 Barua graduated and wanted to go abroad for higher studies, but his mother objected. Apparently she did not want her

[5] Ibid., p. 40.

favourite son to venture so far, but it is also possible that she shared the widespread old belief in eastern India that crossing the seas was polluting. He finally managed to go to England for the first time in 1926, after his mother's death in 1925. While there he was nominated and elected unopposed to the state legislature of Assam. The viceroy, who nominated Pramathesh, was friendly with Prabhatchandra and probably expected his friend's son to be loyal to the Raj in the assembly. But Pramathesh turned out to be a nationalist. He even became the chief whip of the Swarajya Party launched by the freedom fighter Chittaranjan Das. Later he was reportedly invited to join the Assam ministry, but by then he was already obsessed with the idea of making films.

Barua's association with India's nascent film industry began accidentally. He knew film director Dhirendra Ganguli from his days at Shantiniketan. Once, while visiting a film set on the invitation of Ganguli in a Calcutta suburb, he found an actor handling a gun incorrectly. That was one thing Barua knew well; he intervened. The director of the film, Devaki Bose, now requested him to play a small role in the film, which Pramathesh did after initial reluctance.

During a visit to England in 1930, while recovering from an operation to remove kidney stones, Barua went to Paris armed with a recommendation from Rabindranath Tagore and trained in cinematography. He also briefly studied film lighting at Fox Studios during the visit. He came back the same year to found a new film company at Calcutta, Barua Film Unit. Its first film, *Aparadh* (1931), was directed by Devaki Bose. It was the first film in India to be shot in artificial light.

At the time Barua joined the films, the film world was an uncertain marginal culture, ill-defined both in terms of social norms and artistic creativity. He actually joined a group of pioneering filmmakers—directors, artists, writers, musicians, technicians, actors, and actresses—at Calcutta who were then trying to adapt the new media to Indian conditions and taste. The group included persons like Dhirendra Ganguli, Devaki Bose, and Dineshranjan Das. Thanks to such pioneers, films were becoming an important form of mass entertainment in the country, and the various aspects of film-making were opening up new careers for the more daring.[6] But the filmwallahs themselves composed a liminal group at the periphery of society. Barua seemed to like that ambience. Cultural liminality was not unknown to him and gave him a certain confidence in that atmosphere of uncertainty, self-experimentation, and openness. In 1929 he joined the Board of Directors of the British Dominion Films. He first acted in a series of silent films during 1931–2 and, once sound was introduced into the movies, directed the film, *Bangla 1983*, a futuristic fantasy. It was released in a new cinema hall, christened Rupabani by Tagore, but did not do well at the box office.

Though by the end of his life Barua made a large number of movies as an actor–director, for the older generation of Indians his name is associated mainly with eight films: *Devdas* (New Theatres, 1935), *Adhikar* (New Theatres, 1936), *Mukti* (New Theatres, 1937), *Rajat Jayanti* (New Theatres, 1939), *Shapmukti* (Krison Movietone, 1940), *Mayer Pran* (M.P. Productions, 1941), *Uttarayan* (M.P. Productions, 1941) and *Shesh Uttar* (M.P. Productions, 1942). All these had their Hindi versions and reached a pan-Indian audience. Like Ray, Barua was a total director; his camera men and editors were usually a secondary presence in his unit. He wrote his own screenplays and sometimes even the stories. Frequently, he was his own editor and, in one or two cases, his own camera man too.

II

THE BIRTH OF THE HERO

A new world opened up for Barua in 1933 when he joined New Theatres, one of India's most respected film studios. It was

[6] For a charming exploration, in cinema, of the creation of the new profession, see Shyam Benegal, *Bhumika* (Bombay: Lalit M. Bijlani, 1977).

also a studio that 'adopted' Saratchandra Chattopadhyay as its principal literary inspiration and patron saint. Certainly, no other studio was to get so closely identified with movies that were, even when not based on Saratchandra's works, so obviously coloured by his worldview.

Barua's first film under the new banner was *Ruplekha* (1934). The following year he made *Grihadaha*, based on the famous novel of Saratchandra. Both were moderate successes. He really arrived as a major public figure after making *Devdas* (1935) and *Mukti* (1937).

Devdas was a particularly spectacular success and, after its release, both its hero and director quickly became a part of India's film folklore and landmarks in the country's cultural history. In addition to directing the film, Barua played the hero in the Bengali version.[7] The film was made when Barua was undergoing much emotional strain. His tempestuous second wife Amaladevi, better known as Khiti, had just died, and her death was associated not merely with a sense of immense loss but also guilt.[8] Barua could not meet Khiti before she died; he was returning from one of his usual trips to England and his ship reached India a few days after her death. Khiti left behind a small child (who was later on brought up by his first wife, Madhurilata). His letter to his father after Khiti's death is revealing:

. . . you want me to come to Gauripur. I shall not probably come to Gauripur again. I feel ashamed. . . .

[7] He played the role of the heroine's stepson in the Hindi version; Kundanlal Saigal played the hero. The Hindi version was also a super-hit. However, those who have seen both versions will immediately admit that the presence of the hero in the two versions is entirely different. The Hindi version seeks to compensate for the fragile vulnerability of Barua with the help of the magic of Saigal's voice and Timir Baran's music.

[8] Khiti had run away from her home to come and stay with him in utter poverty for a while. She belonged to a landed family which owned the Lakshmipur estate close to Gauripur; Prabhatchandra had reasons to be embarrassed and angered by his son's elopement.

I once told you—and I say so again—life is a gamble. I gambled and lost. Now there is no life; there is only existence.

Diwanji [the prime minister of Gauripur] must have mentioned the matter of my marriage to Khiti. I lost the trust of others when I did not marry her before she bore me a son. That is why I have fallen so low. I have vowed to ruin myself as a penance for that sin.[9]

The same year, Barua learnt he had contacted tuberculosis, then an incurable disease. Presumably he caught it from Khiti, who had died of it. The contagion must have carried special meaning for a person living in a world of sin, expiation and repentance.

This sombre mood was reflected in *Devdas*. Its emotional tone was sharpened by the music of Timir Baran, particularly the haunting songs that Saigal sang for the Hindi version. They took India by storm. For some reason, most viewers saw it as a personal testimony and a confessional. Chidananda Dasgupta says:

He came into his own in the solemn tragedy of *Devdas* (1935). Saratchandra Chattopadhyay had written the novel at the age of 17. It is surprising that this immature piece of fiction should have created such an archetypal hero, a romantic, self-indulgent weakling, who finds solace in drink and the bosom of a golden-hearted prostitute. The character of Devdas has been reincarnated a hundred times in Indian cinema under many guises; its ghost refuses to die. Perhaps . . . the dream of surrendering life's troubles to the solace of drink and the arms of a lover–mother is too attractive an escape to be banished altogether from our secret selves.

Barua was not only the creator of Devdas, he *was* Devdas. That is why the Hindi version looks so drab to anyone who has seen the Bengali version. Apart from being handsome . . . Barua had a tragic, if rather solemn intensity. His voice had depth, and he spoke in a low, understated manner . . .[10]

Bengalis have never drawn a sharp line between cinema and literature. The term for a film in Bengali is *boi*, a book; a film is

<hr />

[9] Letter of Pramathesh Chandra Barua to Prabhatchandra Barua, 31 May 1934, Basu, 'Rajar Kumar', pp. 229–30.

[10] Dasgupta, *The Painted Face*, p. 29.

supposed to narrate a novel, play or *purana* faithfully. This has spawned—film theorists like Dasgupta believe—a cinematic language that is never entirely independent of literature. (The language was to face its first serious challenge from Ray.) One suspects that to the Bengalis at least, *Devdas* was Barua's book of life, perhaps even his autobiography written uncannily before his times by a gifted novelist.

A detailed discussion of *Devdas*—as a novel, a film and as a mythopoetics of the hero—is beyond the scope of this exercise.[11] But is its protagonist only a weakling who finds solace in drink? Or is he one who defies tradition for the sake of romantic love to lose both and then, when he turns to the city as an escape, finds modern urban life a disloyal ally, as heartless as the norms he has disowned? Is the golden-hearted prostitute only a counter-factual rationalization of unacceptable sexuality or is her maternal care an attempt to humanize the seemingly dehumanized, deadening impersonality of civic life? Is the divide between Parvati or Paro (the village girl Devdas loves and loses) and Chandramukhi (the urban prostitute) a divide between the past and the present, between two ways of defining Devdas, between an increasingly distant village and the 'tinsel glitter' of India's now-burgeoning cities offering their versions of social norms? Could Devdas have been something more than the teenaged hero created by a famous novelist in his teens? I shall argue later that Indian cinema still grapples with these questions. The final answers to them are yet to be given.

Devdas must have been many things to many people, but he was above all the first successful hero in Indian cinema who seemed to seriously negotiate the anguish of the first generation of a rural élite entering the pre-war colonial city. His self-destruction bears the imprint of both his ambivalent defiance of the village— to which he tries to return before his death in one last, doomed

[11] For details see Poonam Arora, 'Devdas, Indian Cinema's Emasculated Hero, Sado-Masochism, and Colonialism', *Journal of South Asian Literature*, 1995, 30(1/2), pp. 253–76.

effort to reconnect to a lost past and escape anonymous death in a soulless city—and his final rejection of the urbane charms of a seductive new lifestyle. In India's epic traditions, Chidananda Dasgupta tells us, the happy man is an *aprabasi*, one who is not uprooted.[12] The oppressive village society begins to look different, once Devdas has experienced homelessness in the city. The city loses Devdas and probably does not even notice it; the village cannot own him, even in death. He is mourned, privately and in loneliness, only by two women who serve as the co-ordinates of his torn life—by Parvati, to whom he is the loveable rebel who defies norms only to affirm his higher-order conformity to them, and by Chandramukhi, for whom he symbolizes the squandering generosity of a pastoral prince self-destructively opposing, and thus revalidating, her personal knowledge of the calculative rationality of a bourgeois culture. Both co-ordinates must have made immense sense to an audience facing the problem of refashioning their selves in response to the changing demands of Indian modernization. Both invoke in Devdas nostalgia mixed with ambivalence. Not merely his conservative society but he, too, is unable to own up either of them fully. It is not surprising that 'virtually an entire generation wept over Devdas.'[13]

The making of *Devdas* brought another woman into Barua's life. To play the role of the heroine he chose Jamuna, a woman who had lived at the peripheries of respectability and with whom he had fallen in love. They got married in 1934, when *Devdas* was being made.

In 1937 was released Barua's other great success, *Mukti*. It was produced, directed and scripted by him. The name of the film was

[12] Dasgupta, *The Painted Face*, p. 53.
[13] Eric Barnouw and S. Krishnaswamy, quoted in Arora, 'Devdas', p. 254.

suggested by Tagore who had heard the story from the film's music director Pankaj Kumar Mallick and liked it. Though finicky in such matters, Tagore also permitted Mallick to set to music one of his poems for the film, an unheard-of privilege. The poet also specifically recommended the use of two of his songs for the film.

Mukti was mostly shot outdoors, in Gauripur. A major role in the film was played by Jang Bahadur, Barua's personal elephant. Both were innovations in Indian cinema. Once again there is, in the main protagonist of the film, the same mix of unrequited love, betrayal, transition from the village to the city alongside a doomed attempt to return from the city to wilderness, loneliness born of the inability to handle the impersonal heartlessness of the city, and self-destructiveness. This time the journey from the village to the city is implicit and has already taken place when the story begins. The narrative and the hero's search for freedom begins in the city and ends, as it had to do for Barua, tragically, in the sylvan surroundings of his childhood—in the magical, adventure-infested rain forests of Assam. The hero returns there to seek in nature, and in the forest people, a solace and a respite that he sought earlier from the women in his life. But nature betrays him as decisively as the city and his well-bred, urbane lover; at his moment of death he is left only with the tribal youth he has befriended. As in *Devdas*, even in death he is separated from his estranged lover, but the separation is sharpened this time by his belief that it means freedom for her, for she had felt burdened by his private ghosts. *Mukti*'s hero, too, is the scion of a rural aristocracy, but he is so in the sense in which Barua was one; there is a clear touch of class in him, despite what Dasgupta calls Barua's 'execrable taste', reflected in the paintings and sculptures of the artist–hero.

Mukti's hero too caught the imagination of India's middle classes. He looked like a more modern variation on Devdas and even more like Barua himself. *Mukti* is not merely a story of a self-pitying, rejected lover. It invokes memories of a number of other heroes of Saratchandra, and it does so in a particular way. Its hero spans the spectrum that defined Bengal's middle-brow ideal of a hero—in epics, contemporary literature, art, theatre, and in politics—to give that ideal a more urbane content, without disturbing its psychological moorings. It was as if Barua was determined to take over and embellish, with the help of Saratchandra, what lurked in the heart of the Bengalis and important sections of India's urban, semi-westernized middle classes: the fantasy of an archetypal mother's son perpetually trying to find a touch of uterine warmth and oceanic feeling in his encounters with women and the world, and to recreate situations of grand defeat and personal tragedy which would allow an 'ultimate' woman to enter his life and reinstate a lost, maternal utopia, painted in pastoral shades.

Whatever else this myth did or did not, it consolidated cinema as a form of self-expression in Indian society. It also made Barua all the rage. Not only did he become the most conspicuous symbol of the new art form, he seemed to be living out the myth of the new hero, breaking down barriers between cinema and life, myth and reality, past and present. Even his sartorial style was now copied. People wore Barua jackets, shirts, and collars. Dasgupta describes the bonding between Barua and the Indian middle class in the following words:

No personality in the cinema had established more identity between his private life and the films he created, the roles he played. His films were not objective records or interpretations of the work of others, they were intensely personal. He did not merely make Devdas. He was Devdas.
    Rarely has a filmmaker been as much of a legendary hero as Pramathesh Barua, Prince of Gauripur, Assam. Aristocrat, horseman, marksman, dancer, tennis player, hunter, music lover, foreign travelled actor and director, his image was of an irresistible prince charming descended upon common folk, honouring them by his very presence in their midst.[14]

Between them, *Devdas* and *Mukti* sum up the legend that Barua was, on screen and in life. Both Baruas epitomize paradigmatic journeys, from the village to the city and from the city to

[14] Chidananda Dasgupta, quoted in Barua, 'Pramathesh Barua', pp. 24, 40.

the village. But the psychological geography of these journeys also includes less territorial voyages—from maternity to conjugality to maternity, and from the past to the present to the past. All heroes are defined by their voyages, and Barua too is etched forever in public memory as the first one in Indian cinema who could never return home, who in the final moments of his journey, when he seemed to have made it, was tragically felled by his own character flaws and fate. That his journeys exteriorized the inner journeys of millions in his audience only added to the poignancy of his failures.

Soon after making *Mukti*, Barua left New Theatres—without any obvious provocation. Many of his friends and well-wishers were aghast; others were perplexed, shocked or anxious about his future. Their apprehensions proved justified. Though he made a series of commercially successful movies afterwards, none came anywhere close to capturing the magical effect of *Devdas* and, for that matter, *Mukti*. Till the end, his association with New Theatres remained the most rewarding phase of his life. Though obviously not a non-partisan observer, his one-time mentor Birendranath Sarkar, who headed New Theatres, expresses what many of Barua's friends were to feel about the vicissitudes of his career. While affirming that Barua was a 'true artist', Sarkar says:

However, he was extremely sentimental and egoistic. He left N.T. at the prime of his career. The reason is not known for sure. Perhaps we had unwittingly hurt his feelings. . . . A certain dissatisfaction and melancholy, a secret revolt against society lay buried deep within him. Despite his multiple talents and capabilities, he failed to attain complete fulfilment in his lifetime. This was the greatest tragedy of his life.[15]

Barua's career as a filmmaker was also interrupted by his fragile health. This meant frequent visits to England for treatment—a time-consuming affair in those days. Interruptions also resulted

---

[15] Birendranath Sarkar, cited in Barua, 'Barua'.

from his frequent changes in producers, financial crises, and affairs of the heart. It was a minor miracle that, by the end of his career, he had made so many films, and that so many of them were such resounding hits.

True to his popular image and the lifecycle of some of his favourite heroes, Barua died of tuberculosis. As in nineteenth- and early-twentieth-century England, the disease carried rich cultural meanings for urban, modernizing India. Especially among the Bengali élite, tuberculosis was as much a personal statement as a medical diagnosis. Often associated with a delicate, poetic temperament, it also conveyed waste, self-imposed suffering, reckless surrender to the seductive charms of urban life, doomed or unrequited love. In Barua's case, these associations were strengthened by his suicidal carelessness about his health and the half-heartedness with which he got himself treated in Europe, even when he went there ostensibly for reasons of health. (He used these trips abroad mainly as excuses for travel.) It seemed as if he had accepted his disease as a gift from Khiti and was determined to die as a penance for past transgressions. Even in death, no one could accuse the lost prince, haunted by his inner demons, of deviating from his chosen way of life.

Illness, however, was only a part of Barua's problem in his later years. He had earned and spent money like a gambler prince. Now his recklessness was taking its toll. Even more painful was his loneliness. That, too, Jamuna says, he took in his stride, as the deserved fate of all artists negotiating and surviving on popular taste.[16]

[16] Sandhya Sen, 'Jamuna Devir Chokhe Kumar Pramathesh', *Cinemajagat*, November 1967. Barua's acceptance of the fickleness of public taste might have been less than total. A friend remembers how, on finding out that a very handsome, very old, starving woman begging at the entrance of his studio was

But he did grudge his 'routine existence', despite being fatalistic about it: 'I could not imagine living a mundane and routine existence. Yet now I have been compelled to lead such a lifestyle. This is the irony of fate. I have no regrets about this. . . . I have been defeated in the battle of life and I accept my defeat.'[17]

Barua died in 1951 at the age of forty-eight. He used to say that no one had the right to live beyond the age of fifty. Even in death he had conformed to Saratchandra's—and his own—standards of a tragic, romantic hero.

When he died, Independence had already come, along with massive communal riots, the partition of India, and an exodus involving millions. Bengal was now divided between two brand-new nation-states, with the film studios, professional skills and the producers concentrated in Calcutta, and a majority of the consumers in another country, Pakistan. It was obvious, even to the most obtuse, that Bengali cultural life and Bengali cinema would never be the same again. Whether they admitted it or not, the Bengali middle classes knew that Barua's death symbolized the end of an era. Describing his last journey to the cremation grounds, the distinguished writer Sailajananda Mukhopadhyay said: 'To see him for the last time, every house on the roadside had become a jungle of people; there was not an inch of space anywhere. Behind his flower-adorned dead body were his innumerable, grieving friends. . . . It seemed that everybody in the huge metropolis, old and young, was running out to pay his or her last respect to their beloved 'Devdas'. I had not guessed that he was so popular, perhaps because I was so near to him.'[18]

---

a once-famous actress, Barua gave her his entire month's salary, a princely sum, which he was carrying at the time. But he also warned her: 'If I ever see you here again, I shall shoot you to death.' Prabhat Mukhopadhyay, 'Madhuparka', *Galpabharati*, Puja Number, 1977.

[17] Barua, quoted in Barua, 'Pramathesh Barua', p. 40.

[18] Sailajananda Mukhopadhyay, quoted in *Chalacchitralok*, October 1963.

Mukhopadhyay had underestimated not so much Barua's popularity as the extent to which Barua had come to represent the defeat and demise of Bengal's first innocent affair with the urban–industrial vision. Mourning the death of Barua so spectacularly was one way of expressing the inability to mourn that other death. Barua had lived as if death defined a person in a manner that life by itself could never do. He never knew that his death in turn was defined by a larger, unacknowledged loss of innocence and the demise of a way of life.

III

THE REMEMBERED HERO

Barua was already a legend when he died. Yet, his immense success as an actor–director failed to camouflage the story of dissipation, disorganization, and injudicious emotional investments that his life had become. He *did* give the impression of being a vulnerable, over-protected mother's boy who never grew out of what sometimes goes in India with such vulnerability and protection—a certain non-calculative, self-pitying, adolescent romanticism and self-subversion. Few public figures epitomized so neatly in their personalities the transition from the relatively self-contained world of the traditional landed gentry to the world of modern, monetized, mass entertainment and the demands of urban, impersonal, cosmopolitan living.

Nothing revealed that ability to symbolize the transition more dramatically than Barua's attitude to two major components of the new urban–industrial world he had entered—money and sexuality. He was always uneasy with money; he just could not handle it. In addition to being an expensive producer–director, his style of film-making often involved costly retakes and budget overruns. In a nascent, highly disorganized industry, where financial management was a vital skill, Barua always maintained the touch of a gullible amateur. From an early age he had lived in style; the monthly stipend his family sent him when he was a student at Calcutta was higher than the revenues of many smaller princely states, and in adulthood he earned enormous sums of money as an actor–director. But much of the money went down the drain. Though he never lived in conspicuous luxury—he never used a guard and never had a proper secretary—he was often out of pocket and had to draw upon his family wealth to cope with financial crises. Sometimes even that did not work. Towards the end of his life, his personal finances were in a mess.

What was true of Barua's attitude to money was also true of his sexual exploits. In all, he married four times. (One of the marriages still remains a secret. The details of the marriage, from which he had a son, are not known, except reportedly to one biographer, who has refused to divulge them.) It is said that only his first marriage to Madhuri was a well-considered step, and that too because she had been chosen by his mother after a long search. Madhuri remained steadfastly loyal to him and tolerant of all his aberrations from the conventional idea of an Indian husband. One suspects that she gradually became for her wayward husband a maternal presence, tolerant of his escapades but also firm and protective about her own dignity and individuality. In his other three marriages, he wanted to give social status and financial security to lovers who bore him children. In addition, there were his countless extra-marital affairs, including visits to prostitutes, which he converted into flamboyant, demonstrative affairs of the heart *a la* Saratchandra Chattopadhyay.[19] But he was never comfortable about them either; all of them were sources of misery, especially intense feelings of guilt, and most ended painfully. As he wrote to

[19] See the letter of Pramathesh Chandra Barua to his friend Prafulla Dasgupta, 16 April 1933. Also the letter to his sister Niharbala, 10 April 1933, on his visits to a prostitute and on his romantic, deeply emotional relationship with her. Basu, 'Rajar Kumar', pp. 221–2.

Madhuri after marrying Khiti, 'I had expected not happiness but escape from the hand of my conscience.'[20]

Reading Barua's letters and the reminiscences of those who knew him, one begins to suspect that he was no Don Juan or Giovanni Casanova. Women were not so much objects of conquest for him as lumps of clay waiting to be moulded into something beautiful—physically, socially, aesthetically and intellectually. At least in this area of life, he sought mastery not over inner doubts about his own masculinity, as philanderers usually do, but over a powerful, uncontrollable, natural force that could be shaped into more creative forms. Jamuna relates how reluctant she was as a plain-looking, non-Bengali-speaking woman to enter films, and adds, 'He [Barua] was a creator who experimented with my life. He wanted to know whether he could trace two different entities in the same women. His experiment was successful. He could find Devdas' Paro and his wife Jamuna in one and the same woman.'[21] This search went with somewhat pitiable attempts to get nurture and demonstrative love from all his wives and mistresses. Overtly in the case of the tempestuous Khiti; less directly in the case of Jamuna.[22] But the attempt was, strangely enough, most sustained in the case of his 'abandoned' first wife who emerges from his correspondence and the fading memories of contemporaries as an emotional refuge, source of sympathy and acceptance, and perhaps also as the final judge and arbiter in his battles with himself. When

[20] Pramathesh Chandra Barua, letter to Madhurilata Barua, 16 September 1934, quoted in Basu, 'Rajar Kumar', p. 232.

[21] Barua, 'Pramathesh Barua', p. 38. Was this search for a woman who would be her own double a perennial Indian quest? Why have generations of mythmakers in South Asia grappled with this issue? For a brief discussion of the two aspects of the mythic woman, see Ashis Nandy, 'Woman Versus Womanliness: An Essay in Cultural and Political Psychology', *At the Edge of Psychology: Essays in Politics and Culture* (New Delhi: Oxford University Press, 1980), pp. 32–46.

[22] Ibid.

Khiti left him and took with her their son, it was to Madhuri that he turned for solace and understanding.[23] One is tempted to guess that, in addition to being a nurturing maternal authority, she gradually became over the years, in a peculiar reversal of roles, the reincarnated mother with reference to whom his other lovers had to play out their roles as the Paros or Chandramukhis of his life. He seemed more willing to face social censure than Madhuri's rejection; yet he had to defy her to come back to her.

One thing, however, seems certain. Despite a clear narcissistic strain in his personality, Barua was never calculating in his affairs; they were therefore bound to be self-destructive enterprises in the end. He was ever ready to fall in love, but did not know how to fall out of love. A shy, romantic moralist, with a sense of *noblesse oblige*, he had internalized middle-class values and come to share the fantasies he acted out on the screen. What this ultimate hero of the world created by Saratchandra Chattopadhyay had once said about Devdas remains a vital clue to his own life: 'because the love of Devdas could not transcend the physical, it took him towards destruction.'[24]

As it turned out, it was not so much an impersonal appraisal as a self-fulfilling prophecy. And such was Barua's mythic stature in middle-class India's fantasy life that that prophecy set the norms for an entire generation of great actor–directors of commercial cinema who followed him. This was particularly true of those who, like him, had the looks and personality that conveyed the image of an innocent, artistic dreamer lost in an overly realistic world and waiting to be protected or mothered (the kind of image actor–director Guru Dutt and, less directly, Raj Kapoor, both brought up in the ambience of New Theatres, cultivated, built upon, and died with).

[23] See for instance Pramathesh Barua's letters to Madhurilata of 5 April 1933, 14 August 1933, and 8 May 1934 in Basu, 'Rajar Kumar', pp. 220, 224, 227.

[24] Pramathesh Chandra Barua, quoted in Mukhopadhyay, 'Madhuparka'.

To adapt Ramchandra Gandhi's comment on the theatre, cinema can be subversive in societies where identities have become fixed, for it challenges the rigid boundaries of the self by owing up, temporarily, other identities.[25] In South Asia, where the plurality of the self is culturally given and even celebrated in both folk and classical traditions, cinema's role in society should therefore be more modest. Yet, for those partly uprooted from their traditions and entering the more impersonal urban–industrial culture in South Asia today, the fluidity or play of identities Gandhi talks of might have acquired some radical potentialities.

Every revolution, however, throws up its own versions of triumphalism, self-certain millenialism, and tragic dead-ends. If in colonial India the mythological films showed that Indians could be gods and defy their subjecthood,[26] Barua and his contemporaries, when they broke out of the tradition of the mythological films, showed that the new world India was entering with such innocent enthusiasm could turn, with cannibalistic pleasure, on anyone who did not read all traditional norms and pieties as fatal liabilities.

Looking back, one recognizes that Barua not merely broke the barriers between his personal life and the characters he portrayed on the screen, but also legitimized through the parabola of his personal life the transgressions of the hero who had made the ambivalent journey to the city, without forgiving himself for doing so. Living out his life as an urbane Devdas—whose tragedy he captured for the screen with such moving, if maudlin and self-indulgent elegance—Barua took to a logical conclusion his created persona and his ability to deploy the self-definition thrown up by the entire gamut of heroic characters Saratchandra Chattopadhyay had created. Though Barua once claimed that the characters on screen he had created were inspired by the life around him, the

[25] Presentation at the Seminar on Bhartrihari, organized by the Lalit Kala Akademi at Rabindra Bhavan, New Delhi 1992.

[26] Ibid.

inspiration came filtered through the novelist's imagination.[27] Saratchandra was the one who combined for his protégé aristocratic 'decadence', nineteenth-century romanticism, the pathos of exile from a protected village life, defensive aestheticism and self-destructiveness and, as a psychoanalyst might add, narcissism tinged with unfulfilled oral dependency needs. As an archetypal hero of Saratchandra, Barua *had* to be in constant search for maternal nurture, unconditional love, and firm handling. The women who entered his life seemed eager to meet these needs and the women in his audience were also probably as willing to offer him that mix of nurture and authority in abundance. His fans identified with him not merely because they saw in him their ideal self, but also because their needs coincided.

When the well-known director Bimal Roy remade *Devdas* (1955) in Hindi, with the gifted thespian Dilip Kumar as the hero, he produced, many hard-hearted viewers believed, only a polished, new version of Barua's classic. Roy had been Barua's cameraman and admirer. He knew the power of Saratchandra's myth, which neither the novelist when he wrote *Devdas* nor literary critics took seriously. In the 1950s, as an independent, famous producer at India's new film capital, Bombay, Roy wanted to make full use of that awareness. In its third incarnation, too, *Devdas* was a huge success.

People who had seen all three versions of *Devdas* knew that Roy's version was cinematically more polished than the two earlier ones made by Barua. Dilip Kumar, who had for years specialized in tragedies, put in an excellent performance as Devdas. Post-Independence filmgoers may have sworn that 'Dilip was born to play Devdas';[28] almost no one from the older generation thought so. Certainly no Bengali film critic seemed happy, they praised Roy and could find no major flaw in his *Devdas*, but felt that it

[27] Pramathesh Barua, quoted in Barua, 'Pramathesh Barua', p. 18.
[28] Arora, 'Devdas', p. 263.

had not met the standards set by Barua. As for Dilip Kumar, one critic in a major journal, perhaps not finding good reason to dislike his Devdas, claimed that the actor's overly-mature looks and acting were no match for Barua's slender innocence (*chipchipe saralya*).[29]

For these critics, not only had Barua's life and cinema overlapped, but they also perhaps felt that once he had portrayed and personalized Saratchandra's hero, it was impossible to outperform him. For Barua had taken over, deepened and enriched the Devdas myth; he had lived and died as only Saratchandra and his readers could have imagined. 'Perhaps the whole purpose of your advent in the world of cinema', the novelist himself had said, was 'to give life to my brainchild Devdas.'[30]

IV

THE HERO AS THE AUTHORITY

Let us now return to our original question. Satyajit Ray and Ritwik Ghatak looked differently at Barua because they coped differently with that archetypal hero and the shared fantasies that gave him substance. Ray would have hated to admit this, but many of his own heroes—from the *Apu Trilogy* to *Mahanagar*—can also be read as variations on an archetypal mother's son banished from a flawed pastoral bliss and lost in an urban, impersonal, commercial jungle. Sometimes even when they look very different, as for instance in *Jalsaghar* or *Seemabaddha*, the tensions in their

[29] It is not surprising that when the famous Bengali actor Uttam Kumar was invited to play the title role in a new version of *Devdas* in the 1970s, he refused. He said that he would not be able to equal Barua's performance. Perhaps he sensed that even if he matched Barua's acting, there was little chance of his breaking into the myth Barua had left behind. Perhaps as the other great personification of Saratchandra's hero who had made the archetypal journey from the village to the city, Uttam Kumar felt duty-bound not to poach upon an area marked out as the domain of Barua in public memory.

[30] Saratchandra Chattopadhyay, quoted in Barua, 'Pramathesh Barua', p. 19.

personalities—and the inner contents of their tragedy—either replicate Barua and Devdas or rebel against that stereotype. Even Ray's first story for a film, *Kanchenjunga*, can be read as a story of the same archetypal hero trying to transcend his self, painfully and with an immense effort of will. The protagonists in some of his later works, especially in his highly popular science fiction and crime thrillers, do not follow that model, but Ray himself suspected them to be his lesser creations.[31] Not only are they written for children, their heroes live in a virtually all-male world. The protagonists in these works have no opportunity to sweep their heroines off their feet the way Barua might have done in the case of some of Ray's more consequential heroines. After all Barua did turn many of Ray's own cultural heroes—from Rabindranath Tagore to Saratchandra Chattopadhyay to Bibhutibhushan Bandopadhyay—into his unqualified fans.

Ray's contempt for Barua *was* a defensive manoeuvre, an attempt to cope with the fear of a liminal filmmaker who unwittingly spanned traditional commercial cinema and serious art films by negotiating the common core fantasies of both. Barua was too deeply into Saratchandra and looked too compromised and yet, at the same time, too close to be a comfortable presence. He had taken the first step on the road Ray was to walk but the step was unsure and ungainly. The contempt was sharpened by two other factors. First, there was Ray's self-conscious attempt to defy the established conventions of popular Bengali and Hindi cinema. His realism, his avoidance of the maudlin, his refusal to view cinema as merely a means of visually portraying a novel, and his austerity did not come so much from the masters of world cinema

---

[31] See on this subject Ashis Nandy, 'Satyajit Ray's Secret Guide to Exquisite Murders: Creativity, Authenticity and Partitioning of the Self', in *The Savage Freud and Other Essays on Possible and Retrievable Selves* (New Delhi: Oxford University Press and Princeton, N.J.: Princeton University Press, 1995), pp. 237–66.

as from attempts to produce works that would flout the conventions of popular films made in Calcutta and Bombay. Few represented these conventions more arrogantly than did Barua.

Second, there was the distance between Ray's middle-class, almost puritanical morality (informed with a social realism that supplied the basis of his concept of good cinema as an art meant for the discerning film-viewer, with its own form of classicism) and Barua's amateurish concept of commercial cinema as a popular art form that made its point mainly by touching the hearts of millions. Barua was nothing if not blatantly high-brow in his lifestyle and middle-brow in his artistic tastes. His tiger shoots, domestic elephants, tennis, expensive cars and wines, and harem of mistresses proclaimed social status; his 'execrable taste' in the matter of contemporary art, to some extent even his total immersion in Saratchandra, proclaimed his middle-brow taste. Ray was middle-brow in life and high-brow in artistic taste. To him the belief that cinema was a popular art form was itself an indicator of an earlier, more primitive phase in the history of cinema.[32]

To put it another way, Barua's life and work were a journey through the world created by Saratchandra Chattopadhyay. That world constituted the mythic underground of middle-class consciousness not merely in Bengal but, at least in the inter-war years, the whole of undivided India. Even this story, ostensibly written as a biographical note on Barua, can be read as a counter-factual, psychogeographical obituary on, or an enquiry into, the real-life fate of a hero of Saratchandra. Barua's strengths and limitations were largely those of the novelist; so were the contours of his moral universe. Ray, on the other hand, was a direct product of the world of Rabindranath Tagore. To him Barua, as indeed Saratchandra, was not merely a popular artist with insufficient sensitivity to the classical; Barua's was the model that had to be defied to create a

[32] Ray, 'Atiter Bangla Chavi', p. 38.

space for real cinema in Indian public life. Cinema, Ray recognized, was a medium that could not be as disdainful of cultivated public taste as some other forms of art.

Finally, there was in Barua the same touch of marginality that, unknown to his admirers, Ray had to live with. Born in a naturalized Bengali family known for its enormous contributions to Bengali literary and cultural life—on this half-forgotten, only theoretically significant marginality Ray added his acquired liminality. He started life poorly acquainted with Bengali literature and Indian music and unacquainted with the Indian village life, later so closely identified in world cinema with his films. His familiarity with western literary classics and music, on the other hand, were deep and abiding. As we have seen, he had not even read Bibhuti-bhushan Bandopadhyay's masterpiece *Pather Panchali* when he illustrated a children's version of the novel for Calcutta's Signet Press and got the idea of making a film based on the novel. If anything, Ray was, despite being a part of Calcutta's gentry, in some ways culturally more marginal than Barua. He had reasons to see in Barua a distorted projection of some aspects of his own self.

Ghatak's response was more mixed. Well exposed to world cinema, he rejected the conventions of popular cinema. Yet, under-socialized by global trends, he also celebrated these conventions by working for commercial film directors like Bimal Roy and Hrishikesh Mukherjee, writing highly successful scripts with which the likes of Barua would have been perfectly at home.[33] Ghatak also was loyal to the first identifier of the practitioners of popular arts: he yearned for a large audience. (He once reportedly thought of shifting to television, thinking that the new medium might give him an even larger audience). Above all, as a maker of art films and as one who had followed in the footsteps of Ray, he had to defy

[33] For example, Ghatak wrote the script for Bimal Roy's commercially highly successful *Madhumati* (1958), a typical romantic fantasy, using reincarnation as a leitmotif.

Ray himself. A part of that defiance was the absence of any over-done denial of middle-brow taste in films. Ghatak sometimes used, much less self-consciously than Ray, variations on the model of the hero that Barua projected. But that was not the only model he had. There were others that defied Saratchandra. While the child hero of *Bari Theke Paliya* (1959) is Saratchandra through and through, the hero of *Ajantrik* (1957) or *Jukti, Takko aar Gappo* (1974) is not in Barua's mould, though in the latter he is probably too obviously a defiance of Saratchandra to qualify as 'free' of Saratchandra. However, in neither case was Ghatak burdened by the 'pasts' of his heroes in popular consciousness. Both kinds informed his self-definition as a creative film director and he switched between them with ease. He was never unduly defensive about the novelist's influence; already an entire generation separated the two. Ghatak could, therefore, own up Barua as a part of his cultural heritage.

One final comment. It was by jettisoning Barua's model of the hero that a new generation of commercial Hindi films, *Zanjeer* (1973) onwards, supposedly made their presence felt in the mid-1970s. Amitabh Bachchan, actor-turned-politician-turned-actor, was to typify that genre for millions of Indians. That negation of Barua, though it went along entirely different lines, was as spirited as that of Satyajit Ray. Much has been written on the subject, and one only needs to draw readers' attention to the available works in the area.[34] Yet, despite much talk about a virile industrial man

[34] For a succinct statement, see Fareeduddin Kazmi, 'How Angry is the Angry Young Man: "Rebellion" in Conventional Hindi Cinema', in Ashis Nandy (ed.), *The Secret Politics of Our Desires: Innocence, Culpability and Popular Cinema* (New Delhi: Oxford University Press and London: Zed Press, 1998). For an

supplanting a chocolate-pie, effeminate hero, in this transition from the earlier romantic heroes on the Indian screen to the present breed of tough, modern killing machines,[35] Saratchandra and *Devdas* have not been truly superseded. As I have pointed out earlier, in one blockbuster after another starring Amitabh Bachchan, the hero starts with a personality that is not very different from that of Barua and Devdas, and he is pushed, against his inclinations and will, into becoming a tough, hard-hearted industrialist of violence operating at the margins of law.[36] Circumstances and a new set of villains bring about this change and the audience is left wondering if, once the ungodly are defeated and handed out their just deserts, the hero would have preferred to return to the old self he had reluctantly shed, a self with which only occasionally the heroine, his double and, of course, always his mother, maintain a link. Hence, the nature of tragedy in these films, when it comes, is so different. It is not open self-destruction and passive resignation to fate as in *Devdas* and *Mukti*. It is a form of active intervention in fate that turns physical, hyper-masculine violence into a new form of self-destructive alcoholism and sexual engagement, and makes the conjugality of woman mostly a passive, ornamental presence in a film. It is the self-sacrifice of a person who has been forced into a life of violence and who, while defeating the

---

excellent, if uncritical and frothy treatment of the Amitabh Bachchan genre, see Susmita Dasgupta's unpublished Ph.D. dissertation, Jawaharlal Nehru University, 1993.

[35] Kishor Vallicha (*The Times of India*, 9 September 1979) was probably the first to identify, in the persona Bachchan acquired in the middle of the 1970s, the emergence of the industrial man in the fantasy life of the Indians. Also, Madhava Prasad, *The Ideology of Indian Cinema* (New Delhi: Oxford University Press, 1997); and Kazmi, 'How Angry is the Angry Young Man'.

[36] See also Ashis Nandy, 'Introduction: Popular Cinema as a Slum's Eye View of Indian Politics', in Nandy, *The Secret Politics of Our Desires: Innocence, Culpability and Popular Cinema* (London: Zed Books and New Delhi: Oxford University Press, 1998), ch. 1.

villains in a paroxysm of violence, dies with the dream of returning to his 'normal' self unfulfilled. From *Deewar* (1975) to *Sholay* (1975) to *Mukaddar ka Sikandar* (1978), *Kaliya* (1981), *Shakti* (1982) and *Agneepath* (1990), it is the same story.

3

The Journey to the Village as a Journey to the Centre of the Self

Mrinal Sen's Search for a Radical Cinema

We have seen how, in the early decades of the twentieth century, Indian creativity gave a new epic status to the old journey from the village to the city—from the seemingly familiar, uterine, even if routinely oppressive, narrow fantasy life of the village to what looked like the liberating anonymity and non-traditional vocational choices of the colonial city. As the city became the epicentre of new forms of adventure in ideas and creativity, it also offered to open up the opportunities of defying a conventional, pre-formatted life and experiment with new cultural experiences and with refashioned or extended selves.

We have also suggested that though in pre-colonial India, too, cities were centres of commerce and politics, the ultimate prototype of the journey from the village to the city was probably the journey to a pilgrimage town. This involved the imagery of a hazardous, self-testing, spiritual quest with a built-in routine of return to the village with a less-than-routine consciousness. The fascination of the new journey to the city was that it allowed the hero to discover, at the end of it all, that the city's promise of freedom also camouflaged a certain heartless, inhuman impersonality, casual cynicism, and a persistent quiet violence.[1] The return to the village was, therefore, never routine. Life in the city had to include a dream of return but, as in any diaspora, the dream's haunting quality came from the tacit realization that it had to remain unfulfilled. For the city was a gamble that one either won or lost and an addiction one never fully abandoned. Even after all its tinsel glitter and psychopathic charms were exposed, it retained its seductive pull. We have also seen how this play with the self was immortalized by the likes of Saratchandra Chattopadhyay, whose middle-brow novels turned it into the grand myth of modern India. His own appeal may have faded, but his myth survives in different guises. India's contemporary popular culture—from Raj Kapoor to Amitabh Bachchan—still sometimes has to pay homage to it, through conformity or defiance.

The mythic status of the second journey in the imagination, from the city to the village, is more uncertain. It is relatively recent and probably has no precursor in colonial India. Often acted out in politics and various forms of voluntarism, the journey has not yet acquired epic stature, though it has been crystallizing since World War II as another grand myth in the Indian creative

[1] Lewis Mumford recognizes this experience of loss of freedom in the city, in imagination often a bastion of freedom, when he speaks of 'the myth of city': 'In short, the monopoly of power and knowledge that was established in the citadel,' he says, 'has come back, in a highly magnified form, in the final stage of the metropolitan culture. In the end every aspect of life must be brought under control. . . . The purpose of control, apart from the profit, power and prestige of the controllers, is to accelerate the process of mechanical control itself.' Mumford adds, 'No part of life could escape this general regimentation. Under the peaceful surface and orderly routine of the metropolis, all the dimensions of violence had suddenly enlarged. . . . The metropolis became more and more a device for increasing the varieties of violent experience, and every citizen became a connoisseur in the arts of death.' Lewis Mumford, *The City in History: Its Origins, Its Transformations, and Its Prospects* (London: Secker and Warburg, 1961), pp. 542, 532.

imagination. Appropriately, this imaginary journey has begun to find its most potent expression in cinema and television, quickly becoming the preferred means of popular self-expression in India. Random examples are Ramesh Sippy's *Sholay*, which turned its main actor Bachchan into the archetypal hero of the 1970s and a series of successful commercial films in the 1980s in which the urbane hero goes to the village—out of idealism, political compulsions, the inner need to redress wrongs done to his ancestors, or simply to find himself.

The idea of capturing a fantasy village for the city is not new. In its social relations, the metropolitan slum has often tried to recapture the community life of the village and, once in a while, slipped into being either a faithful copy or a parody of the village. It is usually the saga of an imaginary return to the village that underpins an urban psychogeography in which the village is the location of an irreverent, active, even aggressive renegotiation of unjust social relations and a test of the principles of radical social intervention. The other part of the saga is the romance of the village in the diaspora, unsullied by the grime of everyday village life. The two parts of the saga now jointly sanction a certain ambivalence towards the village as a new pilgrimage where both culture and nature can be worshipped, but not before the venal priests and pestering touts common to Indian pilgrimages have been eliminated.

The growing confidence of the city in its capacity to interpret the village in its own terms only confirms that the Indian imagination of the city is no longer primarily that of first-generation migrants with living memories of the village, nor of hesitant, self-doubting city dwellers. At the same time, the shared imagination of the village within the urban Indian has narrowed; indeed, it has been radically remodelled by the city to serve the city's own needs. The Indian village as the symbol of a tyrannical system that obligingly conforms to nineteenth-century left-Hegelian depictions of feudalism, the Indian village as the obstinate symbol of mindless homicidal patriarchy, the Indian village as the depot of 'pure' environmental–cultural sensitivity and people's critique of conventional development, and, above all, the Indian village as the counter-city and an escape from the city—these are all markers of the changing political–cultural status of the village.

We have followed the vicissitudes of the first journey—the archetypal one from the village to the city—in the life and works of Pramathesh Chandra Barua, the actor–director who in death has become an eponymous figure in Indian film history, and who symbolized the journey to a degree that probably nobody else did. The myth he personified might have been the creation of Saratchandra, but it was Barua who gave the idea of the anguished journey to the city its tragic grandeur. I shall now turn to the second journey—that from the city to the village—through the work of another famous filmmaker, Mrinal Sen, who, unlike Barua, caters to a more exclusive audience in India and abroad. Given the world in which Sen moves, the shift from the first saga to the second is also a movement from more popular modes of self-expression to more sophisticated, self-conscious, artistic self-expression.

The more important difference, though, lies in the collective experiences of uprooting, exodus, and mass death that contaminate Sen's journey. The rigid psychological defences he has built around the ideas of civic virtues, individual creativity, and radical social criticism hide the loss but the anguish occasionally breaks through. Sen cannot be in peace with the city either. The village in Sen's imagination becomes, once in a while, a survivor's village, only he does not acknowledge it. He tries to 'normalize' the loss through his cultivated fear of nostalgia and a radical vision of future that hermetically seals for safekeeping memories of the disasters that have taken place in the past.

I

THE IMAGINATION OF THE CITY

Mrinal Sen, the best known among the living directors of 'art cinema' in India, is usually seen as a chronicler of urban anguish seeking self-expression in doomed violence. This is slightly incongruous. For, though he made his name first as the off-beat director of the selfconsciously international *Neel Akasher Niche* (1958), a somewhat maudlin story of a Chinese hawker in Calcutta, and the artistically more successful box-office failure *Baishe Shravan* (1960), a study in the topography of a marriage disintegrating against the background of the Bengal famine of 1943, outside Bengal the popular imagination remembers him mainly as the maker of *Bhuvan Shome* (1969), a film on the comic journey of an urbane bureaucrat in rural India. Many, including the respected film director Shyam Benegal, consider the film to be a classic that reshaped the idea of popular Hindi cinema.[2]

Sen himself does not seem to rate *Bhuvan Shome* among his best, even though that venture perhaps presaged his most creative phase in the 1980s, when he emerged as a brilliant critic of middle-class life and consciousness and a chronicler of the journey that his society was learning to make some sense of—the journey from the city to the village to the city. Of his films most representative of this phase, at least two are directly concerned with such a journey. As with the journey to the city, this phase too subsumes other kinds of travel—in this instance from the present to the past to the present, and the descent from 'normal', urbane, professionalized public selves into disowned stranger selves identified with the now-shattered community life as it existed till about a generation ago. If Barua's was a journey to the future that turned sour, Sen's is a journey to the past that fails to be therapeutic.

[2] Shyam Benegal, quoted in Deepankar Mukhopadhyay, *The Maverick Maestro: Mrinal Sen* (Delhi: HarperCollins, 1995), p. 67.

In his native Bengal, however, Sen's earlier public image has stuck. It is still that of a radical social critic who made a series of gripping films in the early 1970s, all set in Calcutta. The city was then in the throes of a youthful urban militancy which defied, according to Sen, a tired, hollow 'establishment' unaware that its time was past. These films, which include *Interview* (1971), *Calcutta '71* (1972), *Padatik* (1973), *Chorus* (1974), *Mrigaya* (1976) and *Parashuram* (1978) are all, with the partial exception of *Mrigaya*, portrayals of civic life at a time when, according to Sen, anger had 'thickened in the air'.[3] They are also portrayals of a city which, though structurally linked to the village—as in the moving second story of *Calcutta '71*—is culturally autonomous of the village. Though he claims that in *Padatik* there already was a touch of 'soul searching' and an attempt to 'examine and question' the 'anti-establishment', all the films follow the standard format of left radical-ism known to Indian cinema. However, they became controversial all the same, and Sen admits that he thrived on the controversy.[4]

The angry dissenter, however, acquired an altogether different self-definition and independent voice through *Ekdin Pratidin* (1979), *Akaler Sandhane* (1980), *Chaalchitra* (1981), *Kharij* (1982), and *Khandhar* (1983). *Khandhar* is in Hindi, the rest in Bengali. In these films he seemingly lowers his ambition, cinematically and thematically. His rhetoric does not change and he tries hard to defend his new style in terms of categories derived from his earlier political concerns. Yet his social critique acquires a sharper—perhaps more authentic—edge because of ambitious

---

[3] Of these, Sen does not talk much about *Chorus*, probably because of its overdone cinematographic bravado. Sen himself argues in terms of what he thinks are socio-political categories, such as the establishment and the anti-establishment. I have used them here in his sense. However, his own work suggests that such categories are telescoped deep into each other, so much so that the conventions of one cannot be identified without those of the other.

[4] Mrinal Sen, 'Quite a Few Things about Myself', in Mukhopadhyay, *The Maverick Maestro*, pp. 239–55 (p. 244).

self-explorations and daring attempts to examine the cultural roots and social location of his politics of culture. What was an aberrant, playful, self-exploratory whimsy in *Bhuvan Shome* becomes a serious self-excavation in these movies and, for the first time, Sen hitches his radicalism to a survey of the limits of the moral universe and the shared culture of the makers and viewers of radical cinema. Indeed, all five films transcend the suave radical chic of his earlier cinema which were, to use the expression of anthropologist Trinh T. Minh-ha, 'mainly a conversation of "us" with "us" about "them".'[5] Each has an open-ended, tacit theory of evil, but the evil is no longer located entirely outside; it gets telescoped into the self. Instead of moral self-righteousness, there is in them a quasi-Gandhian awareness of self-complicity and an invitation to a different form of social and political intervention that end up by being a mode of self-intervention, too.

A self-aware filmmaker, Sen sensed that these films were a new phase in his creative life, even though some of his admirers felt that he had 'mellowed' and compromised his Marxism.

In *Ekdin Pratidin* (A Day like Any Other) and in films to follow I . . . pulled my characters by the hair, made them stand before the mirror. They looked into themselves, they confronted the reality, they found no escape route. . . . That was the time when I stopped pointing my accusing finger outside of me.

That was the time when I looked at my enemy inside.[6]

It is not clear how Sen, who had not previously been particularly self-reflexive ideologically, made his shift. Certainly his 'revisionist' vision was not in the air in Bengal at the time, which was dominated by a comic tinsel Leninism, in awe of the ideological frame

[5] Trinh T. Minh-ha, quoted in Linda Alcoff, 'The Problem of Speaking for Others', in Susan Weisser and Jennifer Fleischner (eds), *Feminist Nightmares: Women at Odds* (New York: New York University Press, 1994), pp. 285–309; see esp. p. 286.

[6] Sen, 'Quite a Few Things', p. 247.

built by the Georgian prophet who, alas, like others of his ilk, was no longer honoured in his own land. Sen was never a member of any party but the hold upon him of categories that defined Left-Hegelian praxis in India was deep. Was it Sen's own sensitivities and life experiences that prompted his new experiment with the self? Or was it the inner logic of cinematic creativity that forced on him a new set of choices? Could it be that, having moved out of his economic anxieties and having challenged lower-middle class conventionality, he was now prepared to move out of his lower-middle-class ideas of radical dissent, paradoxically meant for a global audience? Was he looking for modes of social criticism that would make more sense to those inhabiting the world on which he had walked out—the world of his almost-guiltily-remembered, more intimate, early authorities and even god-forsaken Faridpur, the small city in Bangladesh where he was born?

By way of an answer I shall briefly discuss one of these four films, *Khandhar*, which draws, in the starkest possible lines, the contours of Sen's artistic self. I shall do so against the background of both Premendra Mitra's short story on which the film is based and the other film that preceded *Khandhar* by a year and comes closest to it in spirit: *Akaler Sandhane*. My argument is that the imagination of the city that these creative efforts project presumes a counter-imagination distinct from the idea of the village that has dominated middle-class consciousness for generations, and the locus of this new village of the mind has paradoxically shifted to the city. You have to revisit the village as an outsider to make sense of this play of imagination and counter-imagination. First, however, a word on Sen himself.

II

THE LONG SHADOW OF FARIDPUR

Mrinal Sen was born in 1923 and was brought up in his ancestral home at Faridpur, a small town now in Bangladesh. Faridpur had 'a distinctive flavour of countryside' and Sen, devoutly and self-consciously urbane, has always tried hard to turn his back on memories of it. 'Mrinal Sen is . . . chary to talk about his childhood. If one probes hard, he tends to become philosophical. He wants to fight nostalgia because nostalgia leads to sentimentality and sentimentality leads to weakness—he argues with the conviction of a teacher of mathematics explaining an axiom.'[7] Is there something more to this axiomatic rejection of maudlin nostalgia than the fear of 'weakness' he admits? What is this weakness, in any case, and what does living with memories mean to him? Why does he has to declare, even in his seventies, that all his life he has only 'lived in the instant present'?[8] Is Sen, unknown to himself, a survivor like millions of others of the cataclysmic violence that accompanied the birth of independent India? Has he built a defensive shield that protects him from the ghosts of the past? Is his collectivist ideology an effective intellectualization of his minimal self?[9]

Sen now says that his decision to 'abandon' Faridpur was not deliberate,[10] but his distance from the town cannot but be cultivated. It is certainly consistent with some of his known preferences for the civic and the urbane. Thus, he identifies, we are told, not with the child Apu in Satyajit Ray's *Pather Panchali* but with the teenaged Apu of *Aparajito*, wholly alienated from the rural world he has left behind.[11] Likewise, Sen has never felt devastated, as his

[7] Mukhopadhyay, *The Maverick Maestro*, p. 8.

[8] Mrinal Sen, 'Rambling Thoughts . . .', *Social Scientist*, March–April 1997, 25 (3–4), pp. 19–26, see p. 19.

[9] 'Seen through the prism of our contemporary knowledge of radical evil . . . the past evokes nostalgia so intense that the emotion has to be fiercely denied, repressed, and denounced.' Christopher Lasch, *The Minimal Self: Psychic Survival in Troubled Times* (New York: Norton, 1984), pp. 65–6. Lasch also speaks of the survivor's tendency to live in the instant present, to take one day at a time, to avoid 'debilitating nostalgia'.

[10] Ibid., pp. 8–9.

[11] Ibid., p. 9.

friend Ritwik Ghatak was, by his forced separation from his ancestral place. Perhaps for this very reason, Sen has never been easy with the ambivalent, double-edged relationship between the village and the city, specially the haunting persistence of the village in a civic consciousness built on disavowal of the village.

The Sens of Faridpur were an identifiably middle-class, educated, upper caste, Vaidya family. They were also politically alert. In an autobiographical essay, Sen briefly describes his father, Dineshchandra Sen, as a public-spirited, idealistic, reasonably successful lawyer in private practice:

Throughout his career in the courts of law he made his mission to lend active legal support to the militant political activists—'freedom fighters', as they are called now—very few of whom, for obvious reasons could escape death by hanging. My father suffered disbarment for a period of six months when immediately on Mahatma Gandhi's return from the Round Table Conference in England in the early thirties, Gandhiji was arrested and when as a mark of protest my father and his colleagues boycotted the court sessions. On the following day the District Magistrate took his pick, singled out my father and punished him.[12]

The elder Sen was also politically correct:

A year after my birth Deshbandhu Chittaranjan Das came to our small town to preside over the Provincial Ryot Conference—that was C.R. Das's last speech, and my father, in his welcome address as the chairman of the Reception Committee, spoke eloquently about the 'Bolshevik' Revolution in Czarist Russia.[13]

For some reason, the son does not recapitulate here what he says in an autobiographical Bengali essay he wrote soon after British India was partitioned in 1947. The earlier essay is also a

---

[12] Sen, 'Quite a Few Things About Myself', p. 239.
[13] Ibid.

record of his first, painful exposure to the politicization of a socio-
religious schism. In it he tells the story of his close friendship with
Jasimuddin, the famous poet, who later turned into a Muslim
nationalist and got caught in the vortex of communal politics. The
essay recounts that the gifted poet was such a favourite of the
Sens that Mrinal did not know till he was in his teens that
Jasimuddin was not his brother. But the essay also describes
Jasimuddin's occasional arguments with Dineshchandra on the
Hindu–Muslim issue, which sometimes acquired an inflammatory
potential. In these arguments, the young Mrinal often found
his father pleading the case for Hindus and Jasimuddin for
Muslims.[14] They occasionally came close to blows. One biography
also mentions that, at times of communal tension, Sen's 'nationalist
father would develop a streak of Hindu militancy. He would
stockpile bricks, stones and other missiles on the terrace of their
house to be used in case of exigency . . .'[15] Presumably, the elder
Sen's radicalism was tinged with religious nationalism and the
son's defiant turn to ultra-secular, positivist Marxism was not
purely a cognitive choice.

Sen remembers his mother Sarajubala with much fondness:

My mother was a traditional housewife, loving and affectionate, the likes
of whom there were millions in the country. Defying the social
constraints, she once did a bit of a revolutionary job by singing in a
public meeting. It was a Tagore song she sang in a meeting attended by
the famous Bipin Chandra Pal, a stalwart among the then triumvirate
Lal-Bal-Pal.[16]

[14] Dipesh Chakrabarty, 'Remembered Villages: Representation of Hindu–
Bengali Memories in the Aftermath of the Partition', *Economic and Political
Weekly*, 10 August 1996, pp. 2143–61; see esp. pp. 2150–1. Chakrabarty bases
himself on Mrinal Sen, *Chhabi Karar Ager Dinguli*, in Pralay Sur (ed.), *Mrinal
Sen* (Calcutta: 1987), p. 11.

[15] Mukhopadhyay, *The Maverick Maestro*, pp. 6–7.

[16] Sen, 'Quite a Few Things,' p. 239.

She was also a nurturing figure. Her son remembers that Jasimuddin, during a heated debate with Dineshchandra, asked why, if he was considered a member of the family by the Sens, he was served separately. Sarajubala said in anguished, tearful self-defence that the servants, not the householders, objected to a Muslim eating with the family, and she actually had to wash up the utensils herself after Jasimuddin had eaten.[17]

The Sens were not an atypical Bengali, Hindu, middle-class family. They had not lost touch with rural Bengal, but they also had their own distinctive mix of everyday routine, political idealism, and, as one might expect in a colonial situation, a borrowed cocktail of ethnonationalism and radicalism. Above all, it was a family buffeted by the political storms gathering in the subcontinent and trying to make sense of them with the help of often contradictory, arbitrarily chosen fragments of ideologies floating around in the culture of South Asian public life.

In this atmosphere Mrinal grew up among fond parents, brothers and sisters. He was a good student, well read, already at the margins of politics.[18] He also knew he was bright. Indeed, he admits that he was a bit of an egoist and, like many other creative people, felt he was chosen. He once asked his parents whether they considered him a genius. They were taken aback but recovered their breath quickly enough to say 'yes'.[19]

Mrinal's first exposure to cinema was in his early teens when a touring cinema company came to the town. The first film he saw was Barua's *Devdas*; 'he enjoyed every moment of this thrilling

[17] Chakrabarty, 'Remembered Village', p. 2051.
[18] Mukhopadhyay, *The Maverick Maestro*, ch. 1.
[19] Sen, 'Quite a Few Things', p. 239.

experience.'[20] However, his memory of this thrill was ambiguous. One guesses that, as with Ray, Sen's creative style was partly built on the rejection of that early experience of pleasure. He was also getting radicalized at around this time in the company of some of his friends, whom his father, predictably, came to detest.[21]

Sen's self-esteem suffered a severe blow when he went to Calcutta at the age of seventeen to study physics. He enrolled at the Scottish Church College in north Calcutta and decided to stay nearby. His self-confessed 'love affair' with the metropolis, which supplies the background for most of his films, began painfully. Calcutta depressed him and made him feel like an 'outsider'.[22] He was fearful of crowds and found them 'anonymous, self-absorbed, indifferent.'[23] He may have disowned Faridpur, but he carried its imprint. And the departure from and break with the sleepy town marked the end of his childhood and adolescence.[24]

Despite first impressions, Calcutta grew on him, especially as the prism that refracted what he identifies as the three key experiences in his life: World War II, the Bengal famine of 1943, and the communal holocaust in 1946–8. All three disturbed him profoundly but also helped him grow out of his small-town, protected existence and reintroduced him to the times he was living in. As he says, not very originally, it was the worst of times, it was the best of times.

Sen's life-long and passionate affair with Calcutta evidently began at about this time.[25] So did perhaps, unknown to him, a

[20] Mukhopadhyay, *The Maverick Maestro*, p. 4.
[21] Ibid., p. 5.
[22] Ibid., p. 240.
[23] Ibid.
[24] Ibid., p. 8.
[25] Some years ago Sen made a documentary on the city, *Calcutta My El Dorado* (1989), which I have not seen. His ambivalence towards the city may

certain ambivalence. This ambivalence included the insecurity of an outsider trying to integrate in an alien culture of cosmopolitanism by exiling his past or by reading parts of his own self as only a romantic, nostalgic beckoning of the past. As we have seen, even the partitioning of India and the loss of access to his ancestral home did not apparently disturb Sen overmuch. They meant to him the loss of a past that he, in any case, was trying to transcend. Sen's imagination of Calcutta *had* something to do with this rejection of Faridpur and the connotations of predictability and conformism that the small Bangladeshi town, smelling of nearby villages, had come to carry. That rejection *did* power his struggle to found his cosmopolitanism on the ruins of the pastoral that pervaded his home town, and his unresolved, insecure, unrecognized discomfort with parental—read paternal—authority. This discomfort shaped his self-redefinition as a radical social critic. For, like many outsiders, Sen found in his early radicalism not merely an ethical anchor in transitional times, but also an easy analgesic. The ideological frame into which he fitted himself— Leninism—meant in India a hard-nosed, aggressively positivist, bigamous creed, happily married to scientism and historicism on the one hand, and to an urban–industrial vision on the other. It gave Sen, one suspects, what he had been tacitly seeking: a collective, linearized, controllable past that would supplant his personalized, disowned past and thereby help maintain the integrity of his self.

As Calcutta engulfed him, Sen found like-minded friends and moved close to the Indian People's Theatre Association (IPTA), a group that brought together some very creative artists and performers. He was also a voracious reader and made full use of Calcutta's numerous excellent libraries. And, despite his new-found cosmopolitanism, he lived in the more typically Bengali north Calcutta, not in the south Calcutta more favoured by the

---

or may not have come through in the film, but it is certainly obvious in some of his later films.

film crowd and other beautiful people. This vigorous intellectual life, however, had little to do with the various jobs he did to make a living. After leaving college, he worked for more than a decade as a medical sales representative and for a while as a private tutor before finding the opportunity to make a film. During this period he also met and married Geeta Shome, an actress who has often performed brilliantly in his films. Somewhere along the way he also shed his Faridpur accent.

Sen's first film was *Raat Bhore* (1956). Most critics remember it as a self-indulgent venture and a producer's nightmare. Sen hates it. I have already mentioned his second and third films, *Neel Akasher Niche* and *Baishe Shravan,* which established him as a politically alert, albeit commercially risky director. There were also the films he made in the 1960s—*Punascha* (1961), *Abasheshe* (1963), *Pratinidhi* (1964), *Akash Kusum* (1965), *Matira Manusha* (1966) and *Bhuvan Shome* (1969)—which helped establish his credentials as a serious filmmaker. He became a cult figure in the 1970s after the release of *Interview, Calcutta '71* and *Padatik.* They made him, along with Ghatak, an icon of the Left in Indian cinema. Ray had never looked radical enough, and the younger Leftist filmmakers were yet to make their mark. Once Ghatak died in 1976, Mrinal Sen became the elder statesman of radical Indian cinema.

Sen, however, is one of those whose brilliance and spontaneity are products of a long struggle against self-indulgence, self-complacence, and a deep fear of mediocrity. 'Few film directors have been blessed with the mix of spontaneity and deliberateness of Mrinal Sen.'[26] Though reared on a steady diet of tired Leninism, he picked up the saying of an Italian Marxist, Elix Vittorini, who insisted that the point was not to pocket the truth but to chase it.[27] Sen now posed a series of new questions to himself: What *is* radical

[26] Chidananda Dasgupta, *Talking About Films* (New Delhi: Orient Longman, 1981), p. 85.

[27] Sen, 'Quite a Few Things', p. 246.

in Indian cinema and life? And what is fundamental social criticism, beyond the ability to speak 'on behalf of the poor and exploited?' At one time his answers to these questions would have been predictable: he had tried to give voice to the silenced and the throttled. This is a project not unknown to Southern intellectuals. The exploited and the voiceless seem to deserve and invite such ethical gestures and pleas for social justice.

He now sought a second chance to answer the questions and reformulate them for the purpose: Who can speak for the oppressed? Where does political sensitivity begin and moral responsibility end? He would have loved the example given by Linda Alcoff, had he known it:

Anne Cameron, a very gifted white Canadian author, writes several semifictional accounts of the lives of Native Canadian women. She writes them in first person and assumes a native identity. At the 1998 International Feminist Book Fair in Montreal, a group of Native Canadian writers decided to ask Cameron to, in their words, 'move over', on the grounds that her writings are disempowering for Native authors. She agrees.[28]

Why does Cameron agree? Alcoff goes on to argue that 'a speaker's location . . . has an epistemically significant impact on that speaker's claims and can serve either to authorize or disauthorize one's speech.' Also,

. . . not only is location epistemically salient, but certain privileged locations are discursively dangerous. In particular, the practice of privileged persons speaking for or on behalf of less privileged persons has actually resulted (in many cases) in increasing or reinforcing the oppression of the group spoken for. . . . Cameron's intentions were never in question, but the effects of her writing were argued to be counterproductive to the needs of Native women because it is Cameron who will be listened and paid attention to.[29]

[28] Alcoff, 'The Problem of Speaking for Others', p. 285.
[29] Ibid.

Mrinal Sen's response to these reformulated questions is indirect and has to be teased out from his work. I shall try to tease them out with the help of one of his most self-exploratory films. However, I shall first look at another film that was his first genuine attempt to write a cinematic autobiography. This is a film that openly sheds not merely the format of standardized radicalism but also the historical consciousness and the stylized patterning of memories and anti-memories which went with the radicalism. The change was to pay him immense dividends as a filmmaker but would bring home to him his homelessness. He does mention 'a terrible sense of emptiness' and 'alienation' at the end of his most creative phase, which later films like *Antareen* reflect.[30]

III

A JOURNEY TO THE VILLAGE
AS PAST

Akaler Sandhane (In Search of Famine) takes Sen back to a theme that first surfaced in *Baishe Shravan*—the man-made Bengal famine of 1943.[31] A film unit wants to shoot a movie on the famine and chooses as its location a village that had been, unknown to the unit, devastated by the famine fifty years earlier. The moviemakers in the film are not the usual glamorous, self-obsessed lot from the film world. They are obviously well meaning, socially sensitive, and try not to be cut off from the village life. They are also friendly and the leader of the team, the film director, is politically alert. So is the heroine, Smita Patil, the famous actress who plays herself in the film.

Even then the team arouses deep anxieties and is unable to control the emotions it kindles in the village. For the very act of going

---

[30] Sujay Dhar, 'Padatik', *The Hindustan Times*, 12 June 1998.

[31] Mrinal Sen, *Akaler Sandhane* (Calcutta: D.K. Films, 1980), Story: Amalendu Chakraborty.

from the city to the village, to make a movie on a trauma through which the village has passed, opens up old anxieties and wounds. As the filmmakers find out to their cost, the famine is not a distant memory but a living reality. Those who profited from it and those who were its victims remain a part of the village. The director finds this out the hard way when an actress contracted to play a role in the film leaves the unit in a huff. When he explores the possibility of casting the star-struck daughter of a village notable in the role, that of a famine victim who turns prostitute, some of the village elders take advantage of his *faux pas*. They whip up emotions against the unit. Though it has come to enjoy the support of the villagers who have been direct or indirect victims of the famine and are happy that the film seeks to document their suffering the unit finds itself reduced to a group of hapless outsiders. It has to leave the village, the shooting incomplete, its allies in the village stranded.

Akaler Sandhane is thus a journey from the city to the village to the city that becomes a journey to the past before the unbelieving eyes of the main protagonists. Sen returns through this journey to one of the three traumas that have shaped his life, the Bengal famine of 1943. It is a return to a puzzle that has dogged the steps of Bengali radicalism for fifty years: a famine in which about four million people starved to death, fifty thousand of them in the city of Calcutta, without any overt resistance or violence whatsoever. The victims seemingly took their suffering as an act of fate and the concerned citizens of Calcutta, unable to seriously intervene, had to pretend to the same fatalism. The film suggests that though the victims did not rebel at the time, they have not forgotten the experience either. Nor have they forgotten those who were culpable and built their fortunes on the plight of peasants willing to sell their land or bodies for a trifle. There is a scene in *Akaler Sandhane* where a character in the film within the film offers to buy land from a starving peasant so that the latter might migrate with the proceeds of the sale to Calcutta and benefit from the free kitchens being run in the city. Both the onlookers viewing the shooting *in* the film and the audience *of* the film know exactly what is in store for him.

The limits of middle-class social awareness is the focus of the story. The incomprehension and the impotence of a film unit devoted to understanding and 'narrating' the famine and intervening in the social processes to which it is witness is part of a larger incomprehension and impotence. The film director and his entourage may not be narcissistic in the conventional sense, but they are so as a social class. Sen invokes two incommensurate worlds in which the polarities are not the oppressor *versus* the oppressed but exploitation, betrayal and victimhood on one side, and distance, cognitive failure and spectatorship on the other. For a brief while, an autobiographical character, the director of the film within the film, transcends that incommensurability. But it is only a passing moment.

The same incommensurable worlds and their brief, cross-mirroring encounter through a hero bearing the burden of his private passions are the stuff of *Khandhar*.

The mythic journeys of the heroes of major epics of the world almost invariably become simultaneous, parallel journeys to the centre of the self. This awareness is now a cliché and a part of the structure of global commonsense. We are all students of myth nowadays and we are all too aware that his journey gives the hero an opportunity to establish his heroic self by confronting external threats—from larger-than-life enemies and overwhelming challenges posed by fate—and by testing out the range and limits of his self. This is as true of the Indian epics as of the Greek. During his exile, Arjuna in the Mahabharata undertakes a series of journeys that explore the frontiers of his gendered Kshatriya self. At different times, he takes the disguise of a dance teacher, an eunuch, and even a lowly charioteer. Rama's journey through his exile in the Ramayana not merely tests the limits of his valour and marital fidelity but also bares his ambivalent relationship with his wife and brother.

The journey of the hero of *Akaler Sandhane* is, in this respect, only a partial exile; it is brief, poignant, and only apparently self-enhancing. It does not truly extend the boundaries of his self; it reveals to him the limits of his emotional reach and depth and the narrow range of his heroic, dissenting self. Only in that ironic sense is the journey one of self-discovery and self-awareness.

Sen's autobiographical journey seems complete in *Akaler Sandhane*. Yet he was not satisfied, evidently. Perhaps the film's story and treatment were not strong enough to carry the burden of the archetypal journey he was dealing with. So, after a brief sojourn he returned to the theme in his next venture *Khandhar*. This time the film was based on an evocative story written, uncannily, half a century earlier by another highly creative, urban Bengali who had sensed the impending demise of the imagination of the village and the growing distance between the reality of the village and the imperatives of civic life.

IV

THE FEAR OF NOSTALGIA

Khandhar (Ruins) is in Hindi, a language with which, despite his three films in it, Sen's skill is uncertain.[32] Perhaps the language helps the director to distance himself from themes that would have been otherwise too frankly autobiographical. It is one thing to decide to be self-critical and self-exploratory and another to be so without being defensive.

---

[32] Mrinal Sen, *Khandhar* (Calcutta: Babulal Chokhani Productions, 1983).

The script is based on a famous Bengali short story of Premendra Mitra, *Telenapota Aviskar* or 'The Discovery of Telenapota'.[33] Mitra's village of imagination, though located near Calcutta, might have conveyed other meanings to Sen. Telenapota is a particularly modest Bengali name for a village that seems to flaunt with a vengeance its humble stature. The story had spawned a Bengali film by writer, painter and filmmaker Purnendu Patrea years earlier, but that effort did not leave much of an impact.

The original story, a masterpiece of world literature, invokes a lost, defeated world and a momentary, unsuccessful attempt to connect to it. It is a story of the past, written paradoxically in the future tense, which gives it a strange touch of timelessness. Also, in a remarkable twist, the language and format successfully abolish the difference between the main protagonist and the reader. Indeed, it is a rare work of fiction in which the reader is the hero. To facilitate this identification, the hero remains nameless throughout. Mitra's story begins:

During the conjunction of Saturn and Mars—yes, Mars, most likely— you, too, might discover Telenapota . . . When you have unexpectedly been granted a two-day break from the suffocating pressure of work, if someone comes and tempts you, saying that somewhere there is a magic pool filled with the most incredibly simple-minded fish anxiously waiting to swallow any bait, and you have often spent unsuccessful hours angling without a catch, you may suddenly find yourself on your way to discovering Telenapota.

To discover Telenapota you will have to catch a bus packed with countless people late in the afternoon, and suffer the crowds, the jolting, the heat till, by the time you get off an hour or two later, you are drenched in sweat and covered with dust. You will be quite unprepared for the stop when it comes. Before you know where you are, the bus will have disappeared into the distance, over a bridge across the low

[33] An English translation is available in Premendra Mitra, 'Discovering Telenapota', in *Snake and Other Stories*, trs. Rina and Pritish Nandy (Calcutta: Seagull, 1990), pp. 1–10.

swampland. . . . You will feel a strange dread slowly rearing its head out of the lonely marsh.[34]

If you are a South Asian, constantly exposed to astrology of all hues, the bitter sarcasm of the first sentence of the story tells it all—that the journey is ill-fated, that the discovery of Telenapota cannot but end in disaster for you, that you will at the end have to rue the discovery and acknowledge that it need not have been made.

In Sen's version it is the story of a middle-class, urbane photographer's journey to a village. Unlike in the original story, he has a name, Subhash, and also a profession close to that of a film director. This is deliberate; Sen is aware of its autobiographical implications.[35] Subhash, with his friends Dipu and Anil, goes to spend a weekend at a village where Dipu has an ancestral house. Though the three friends think of the journey as a weekend excursion, and a break from the predictability and routine of the city, to the photographer it is also a semi-professional expedition. When they reach the humble village dominated by the ruins of a once-glorious, palatial, ancestral house, Subhash encounters in one wing of the house two of Dipu's distant relatives—a blind and dying old aunt and her young daughter, appropriately named Jamini (night). They live in the dilapidated, disintegrating mansion, smelling of decline, decadence and death.[36] The ruins of the house in which the mother and the daughter live are also the ruins

---

[34] Ibid., p. 1.

[35] Mukhopadhyay, *The Maverick Maestro*, p. 157.

[36] Like Satyajit Ray in *Jalshaghar* (1958) and true to the tenets of mainstream Bengali radicalism, Sen has to equate the decline of the Indian village with the inevitable decline of a feudal lifestyle. He also has to introduce in Mitra's story a father and a daughter as domestic helps of the besieged family. They are the only ordinary villagers one meets in the film. Sen is able to empathize with personal tragedies, unfolding as a consequence of large-scale social changes, only as unavoidable costs and markers of a less than tragic passage of an age and social system towards which one could at best be ambivalent.

of their life and the village, and as Jamini moves around the damp, decomposing home of a once-prosperous family, she seems to sleepwalk through life.

In course of the weekend Subhash accidentally gets involved in the lives of the two lonely women. As much out of curiosity as courtesy, he joins Dipu to pay a visit to the two and discovers that Dipu's aunt is waiting forever for the mythical return of one Niranjan who has promised to marry Jamini. Jamini knows Niranjan will never come, for he is already married and well-settled in life. But she also knows that the news will kill her mother, who lives in hope of Niranjan's return. The blind aunt mistakes Subhash for Niranjan and, given the circumstances, Subhash just cannot disown that imposed identity: he finds himself pretending to be Niranjan. He suspects that he may not live up to the promise implicit in that assumed identity, but in that suspicion there is also a touch of ambivalence. Jamini of course knows that the return is fake. But she hopes against hope that there might be a 'return' of another kind, because there has grown a vague, unspoken bond between her and Subhash. For Subhash, that bond is a minor variation on his sense of protectiveness towards the isolated, impoverished family facing destruction; for Jamini it is an unexpected encounter with life, a possible window to a freedom that might also bring with it escape from the poverty, drudgery, and depressive predictability of everyday life. At another time and at another place, they might have fallen in love.

Once again, a doomed relationship underscores the discontinuity between two psychological worlds. These worlds briefly meet, but once the urban protagonist departs at the end of the weekend, they revert to incommensurability. Though there are vague hints that Jamini's world might have been that of Subhash, that his attraction for her is also an attempted return to a now-lost self and a lifestyle on which he has walked out, that connection ends up acquiring only a dream-like quality when remembered through malaria-induced high fever in the original story, and through objectifying photographic records in the cinematic version. Subhash could have ended up by defending his decision to break with the memory of Telenapota by borrowing words from his creator—doing anything else would have been only a nostalgic return to a disowned self, possessing only sentimental value. He knows that when he walked out of that life years ago, he also walked out on a self bracing that life. The weekend has only been an imaginary journey back to the village; in reality, there can be no return, for he has already made his choice and exported the living reality of Telenapota to the past. For a person 'living altogether in the present',[37] all return to Telenapota, like that to Faridpur, could only be a romantic self-indulgence, tinged with a comfortable sense of loss, empathy or pity. The obverse of this is the awareness that, in this archetypal journey, he might have been more real to Jamini than she could ever be to him.[38]

In the Mahabharata, while training with Parashurama in the art of battle under the assumed identity of a brahmin, Karna's disguise is blown and his Kshatriya self is revealed when he bears immense pain to make sure that his guru's sleep is not disturbed. The guru immediately suspects that he is a Kshatriya, not a Brahmin. The Mahabharata does not say if the guru's suspicion triggers doubts in Karna's own mind about his origins and selfhood. In Sen's story of inner exile, Subhash's disguise is blown to him when he tries to convert the promise inherent in his momentarily assumed role as Niranjan into the tame memory of a half-hearted attempt to help a woman caught in an impossible situation. What could have been

[37] Dasgupta, *Talking About Films*, p. 8.
[38] The painful awareness of this asymmetry not only gives *Khandhar* and *Akaler Sandhane* their touch of pathos, but distinguishes them from the other films in the series.

a breakthrough becomes only a remembered break from the normal and the orderly.

When the inevitable happens and Subhash returns to the city, the rupture is made less painful for him by his specialist skills. For he can store the memory of the village, the family, the brief sojourn, and even the haunting beauty of the abandoned young woman in his photographs. What completes the journey is its record in the form of an impressive portrait of Jamini hanging on the wall of his studio in the last scene of the film. Her memory is not commercialized, as one critic alleges. She survives in the hero's world the only way that would allow her to survive—as a two-dimensional reality, serving as a historical record.

The film thus sharpens a question at the heart of the original story: Did the hero ever undertake the journey? Or was his only a weekend expedition pretending to be—or slipping inadvertently into—the metaphor of a nostalgic journey to an ethereal village that would wash clean the discomforts of owning up that life seriously? Would owning up Telenapota have been a case of doomed romanticism or the opening up to an alternative form of realism? The film acknowledges that the hero's journey to the village cannot but require the concurrence of his civic sensitivities; that he will have to, at some stage or other, carefully export to the past the village that lives here and now, only a few miles away from the city.

At the end, this time travel also ensures that, for each of the protagonists, the journey carries a different imprint of reality. For the two friends of Subhash, it has been a matter of a weekend. For Jamini, it might have been a transient but real hope of emancipation. For her mother, it was indeed an emancipatory weekend; the pretence of Subhash gives her a longer tenure of life. For the hero, the journey should have enriched life, giving it the magical touch of a remembered village that is also a remembered affair, but his rational civility intervenes. He has to cauterize the memory by dissociating it from his self as unreal and hallucinatory. In the original story, no doubt is left on this score. The reader as the hero knows that the rupture is complete:

Even after you get back to the city, with its hectic pace and harsh lights, the memory of Telenapota will shine bright in your mind like a star that is distant and yet intimately familiar. A few days will pass in dealing with petty problems, with the usual preoccupations of the commonplace; and even if a slight mist begins to form in your mind, you will not be aware of it. Then, just when you have dismissed all the minor obstacles and have prepared to go back to Telenapota, you will suddenly feel the shivering touch of the oncoming fever. Soon the terrible headache and the fever will be upon you and you will wrap yourself in blankets. . . . The thermometer will register 105 degree Fahrenheit and the last thing you will hear before passing out will be the doctor asking, 'Where on earth did you pick up malaria?'

It will be many days before you are able to walk out of the house and sit in the sun, weak and exhausted by the long fever. Meanwhile, unknown to yourself, your mind will have undergone many changes. Telenapota will have become a vague, indistinct dream, like the memory of a fallen star. Was there ever such a place? You will not be sure. That grave, austere face; those sad and distant eyes; were they real? Or was she, too, like the shadows of Telenapota's ruins, just another unreal, misty dream dreamt in a moment of weakness?[39]

In Mitra's story, descent into high fever distances and dims the memory of a humble village and the two beleaguered women who had hoped against hope. Telenapota becomes in the story a re-membered delirium. In the film, the photographer—I almost said the film director—does so less dramatically, but as effectively, by hanging in his studio a professionally composed photograph that elegantly captures Jamini's distant melancholy. Memory mounted and framed could be as effective an analgesic and amnesiac as malaria.

In both cases, 'Telenapota, discovered for one brief moment, will sink again into the timeless dark of night.'[40]

[39] Mitra, 'Discovering Telenapota', p. 10.
[40] Ibid.

4

The Invisible Holocaust and the Journey as an Exodus

The Poisoned Village and the Stranger City

This is not an age of epics. Epics require epic battles and epic journeys, or at least the capacity to envision them. Indian conventions also insist that such battles should ideally be between persons, clans, or communities close to each other, for only such nearness can ensure that the climactic war will be fought with passion at the margins of morality. The past one hundred years have been a century of dispassionate, well-organized, technicized carnage. They can be the subject of a scientific treatise, not an epic. According to D.R. Nagaraj, by the Indian conventions of epics, the modern West came closest to producing an epic only in the proceedings of the Nuremberg trial after World War II.[1] This was perhaps because the trial brought out, however indirectly, the Dostoyevskian passions that had been missing at Auschwitz, Dachau, and Bergen-Belsen.

Epic journeys, too, have been scarce in this century. As the world has been surveyed and re-surveyed, the sense of adventure

[1] D.R. Nagaraj, 'Ethics and Aesthetics of Representation of Violence', Indo-French Colloquium on Representations and Uses of the Sense of Belonging, Centre for the Study of Developing Societies, Delhi, 1–2 November 1995.

and glory has begun to attach more to the speed and technique of the journey, less to its geography. The only journeys that have acquired heroic proportions in our times are the ones that have sought to alter the cartography of the self. Ours is the age of *Homo psychogeographicus*. At one pitch of discourse, probably the greatest circumnavigators of the earth in this century have been Sigmund Freud and Mohandas Karamchand Gandhi. For both, all great journeys begin when one closes one's eyes and looks within. All landscapes are, by definition, landscapes of the mind.[2] The point of departure for them is self-exile and the crucial mileposts—the ones that tell one whether it is a journey into madness or out of it, whether it is time travel towards the future and self-actualization or towards the past and defensive stupor—are not placed predictably along a road. They too are a matter of discovery.

If the Nuremberg trials can be read as the rudiments of a possible western epic, the closest any South Asian event comes to being the stuff of an epic in the twentieth century are the great Partition massacres and uprooting that took place in 1946–8, when the British empire was being wound up and new states were being created in the region. It involved a journey through violence that would have tested Freud, as it tested Gandhi and, finally, ended in his assassination. Indeed, the events have already written themselves up as an unwritten epic that everyone in South Asia pretends does not exist but are nonetheless forced to live by. That tacit epic, in itself a journey into the self, tells of great battles involving not only valour and sacrifice, but also psychopathic violence, sheer pettiness, and great betrayal. Such an epic dissolves the heroic and the anti-heroic, somewhat in the manner in which the great Mahabharata war did. At the end, once again as in the Mahabharata, we are left with fragments of the hero and the anti-hero distributed over religions, languages, cultures and regions. The listener has to

[2] Cf. S. Schama, *Landscape and Memory* (New York: HarperCollins, 1995).

reassemble the pieces to construct a private ballad, knowing fully that it can only sound like an elegy to some others.

At the heart of that unwritten epic, there is a great journey to exile, too. That exile lasts not for a decade or two; it ensures a lifetime of homelessness. Suketu Mehta unwittingly acknowledges the presence of that unwritten epic when he writes, 'There are millions of Partition stories throughout the subcontinent, a body of lore that is infrequently recorded in print or on tape, and rarely passed on to the next generation. All over the map of the subcontinent, there is an entire generation of people who have been made poets, philosophers, and storytellers by their experience during the Partition.'[3] This is a glimpse into that unwritten epic, getting more tattered everyday in the minds of the survivors, perpetrators, onlookers, and chroniclers. I bear witness to it without reading it the way those who have lived by it may like me to.

I
THE OTHER JOURNEY

Public memory identifies India's day of freedom with tens of thousands of people thronging the centre of New Delhi, Nehru's stirring call to the world in a midnight session of Indian Parliament to acknowledge India's 'tryst with destiny', and the ritual lowering of the Union Jack after two hundred years of British imperial rule. On 15 August 1947 India walked towards a new dawn of freedom; its journey towards nationhood and statehood had begun.

It is in the social sciences, literature, and cinema that beginning and journey have been repeatedly documented and celebrated. They dominate official India even more decisively. Freedom as an event and as an unfolding process is seen as part of a longer journey

[3] Suketu Mehta, 'Partition', *Communalism Combat*, April 1998 (420), pp. 8–12; see esp. p. 12.

towards modernity and progress that began more than 150 years ago in India and is still continuing. Indeed, the idea of that journey has framed the Indian imagination so securely that all social, cultural, political and economic experiences of the country are now seen through it. In what is arguably the most influential popular film made in independent India, *Mother India*, in the penultimate scene the long-suffering, widowed heroine shoots one of her two sons when he is about to abduct a young woman from her own village.[4] That climactic scene seems to crown her lifelong suffering, sacrifice for the sake of her children, struggle against local tyrants, self-denying courage and her allegiance to the community. But that is presumably not enough either for the makers of the film or the audience. For the life and deeds of the heroine have to be fitted—in a social-realist style imported from the erstwhile Soviet Union—within the frame of the official journey on which India has embarked. In the last scene, she—old, venerated and, as the title of the film attests, symbolizing India herself—inaugurates, of all things, a brand new water-management system.

However, there is also the other journey Indians do not like to talk about. That journey, closely associated with the birth of India and Pakistan, also frames significant aspects of the political cultures and international relations of these countries, though it does so silently, without anyone seriously admitting or denying it.[5] The journey began with a massive riot in Calcutta in August 1946 that killed around 5,000 and more or less ended in the end of the winter of 1947–8, after another large riot at Karachi and the assassination of Gandhi at Delhi. The ultimate symbol of the journey was the mass exodus of minorities from the new states that began at some places even before the states were in place. On a rough estimate, 16 million people lost their homes by the beginning of 1948. Many more millions were to be uprooted in the next few

---

[4] Mehboob Khan, *Mother India* (Bombay: Mehboob Khan, 1957).
[5] Ashis Nandy, 'Too Painful for Words?', *The Times of India*, 20 July 1997.

years. It was a kind of journey that South Asians had not previously seen. It uprooted people from habitats they had known for centuries, perhaps even for thousands of years. Yet they considered themselves lucky that they were not among the one million killed. (This is the conservative official estimate. Unofficial estimates mention much higher figures.) As an informant said to historian Gyanendra Pandey, 'It was only in the bloodshed of Partition that ordinary people saw the shape of independence.'[6]

Many of the victims did not even know the larger causes for which they were the sacrificial victims. Nighat Said Khan and Anis Haroon interviewed 100 women in urban and rural Sind and Punjab, Pakistan.

Only the 10 women with professional backgrounds said that they made a conscious decision to come to Pakistan. The rest did not come to realize a dream, but fled instead.

Some were even unaware of Pakistan until some years after its creation. Almost all had never heard of the Muslim League, or the movement for Pakistan and only four from urban Sind and one from rural Punjab had worked for it.[7]

The exodus effectively reduced the number of Hindus in West Pakistan from something like 20 million down to 250,000, nearly all of them in Sindh. Punjab and the North West Frontier Province became virtually free of Hindus and Sikhs. In East Pakistan, it reduced the proportion of Hindus from about 29 per cent to 12 per cent.[8] Moni Chadha, a former diplomat, rightly asks: 'Was the

[6] Gyanendra Pandey, 'Partition and Independence at Delhi: 1947–48', *Economic and Political Weekly*, 6 September 1997, 32(36), pp. 2261–72; see esp. p. 2262.

[7] Nighat Said Khan, 'Identity, Violence and Women: A Reflection on the Partition of India 1947', in Nighat Said Khan, Rubina Saigol and Afiya Shehrbano Zia (eds), *Locating the Self* (Lahore: ASR, 1994), pp. 157–78; see esp. 158–9.

[8] Gowher Rizvi, 'Constitutionalism: The Experience of Bangladesh', lecture at the India International Centre organized by the Law and Society Trust, Colombo, 4 August 1997.

elimination of Sikhs from Pakistan in 1947 the clearest and least acknowledged case of genocide in history? Probably. Why is it that international do-gooders from various NGOs who profess to catalogue cases of genocide and wag accusing fingers about them at international fora never spoke about it for half a century? Why the selective amnesia?'[9] The answer is not available to Chadha because he does not seek clues to it in the tricks his own memory plays with him. Being blessed with a diplomat's perspective on human tragedy, he forgets that, along with the Sikhs, almost the entire Punjabi Hindu community was eliminated from West Pakistan and nearly the entire Muslim community from what was the former East Punjab.[10]

The exodus in north India often took spectacular forms; in Punjab caravans of refugees escaping from the carnage and the plunder sometimes stretched for miles. At places it turned pathetically low-key, too, as in Bengal and Bihar, where tens of thousands of poor peasants and artisans trudged their way towards the newly created borders. At both places they used every mode of transport available—planes, ships, trains, bullock carts, camels— but most of them simply walked to the borders in enormously long *kafilas* or columns. Observers talk of four- or five-mile long columns which, in turn, attracted marauders eager to plunder not only the often pitifully small amounts of belongings the refugees could carry but also the young women among them.

[9] Moni Chadha, 'Partition: A Surgery sans Anaesthesia', *The Hindustan Times*, 31 August 1997.

[10] Mr Chadha does not even care to read the reports of the government he has served. On the basis of the evidence of nearly 15,000 witnesses, given before the Fact Finding Organization set up by the Government of India, Justice G.D. Khosla notes the evacuation of almost the entire Muslim population of East Punjab and concludes that the loss of Muslim life was not less than the loss of non-Muslim life. G.D. Khosla, *Stern Reckoning: A Survey of the Events Leading up to and Following the Partition of India* (1949; rpt. New Delhi: Oxford University Press, 1992), especially ch. 7.

Pandey draws our attention to the memories of one who watched such a column of Muslim refugees going from Kapurthala to Jullunder:

The column was guarded by a few military sepoys. It was ten or twelve deep, the women and children walking in the centre, flanked on either side by men. Groups of armed Sikhs stood about in the fields on either side of the road. Every now and again one of these groups would make a sudden sally at the column of Muslims, drag out two or three women and run away with them. In the process they would kill or injure the Muslims who tried to resist them. The military sepoys did not make a serious attempt to beat off these attacks. By the time the column arrived at Jullunder almost all the women and young girls had been kidnapped in this manner.[11]

II

THE SILENCE OF THE JOURNEY

Few talk about this journey or the events that precipitated it, either in South Asia or elsewhere. In a century of mass murders and massive dislocations, reports of carnage and uprooting too have a diminishing appeal after a while. Nothing could be staler for the media than a repetition of yesterday's events. Also, in a region where life expectancy is still around sixty, many of the victims are already dead. Those who live are often unwilling to talk about their ordeal; they have been silent for years and have seemingly got accustomed to it. Some, after years, have made a reasonable compromise with the past. They too are reluctant to talk. In Pakistan, this 'eerie' silence has become a joint venture of the victims, the historians and the state.[12] It is not the silence of unconscious memories; it is the silence of a secret self.

Many victims call the carnage and the exodus a period of madness. This helps them locate the violence outside normality and

---

[11] Khosla, *Stern Reckoning*, p. 289.
[12] Khan, 'Identity, Violence and Women', p. 157.

disown their memories. Others call the period evil, when all humanity and all ethical concerns were jettisoned. They prefer not to recount those evil times lest they contaminate their new life. The spirits of the victims and perpetrators, they fear, will enter the life of the living if clandestine memories are reactivated:

Daughter, why talk about evil days? In our religion it is prohibited to even utter or think about evil acts. If you do so, it is like actually committing the acts. . . .

If one discusses such acts, one also internalizes them in one's blood and bones . . . There's a saying that if you discuss ghosts and snakes, they tend to visit you. This talk is about dead people. Why invite their ghosts? . . . such talks create a lot of pain and stress. I do not like to discuss them. When we had just come here, we the women used to cry a lot, and exchange stories of misfortune with other families in the camp. But today after fifty years, the wounds have healed. Why are you stoking them?[13]

Yet, at the same time, there is anger and hurt in the victims that their suffering has not been fully acknowledged. After arguing that Partition violence should not be remembered, one survivor says, 'I do not understand, what I should tell you, and to what extent

---

[12] Khan, 'Identity, Violence and Women', p. 157.

[13] Meenakshi Verma, Interview with Rajinder Kaur, February 1997. The interviewee adds: 'By the grace of Vahe Guru, we are quite comfortable . . . and do not need anything. The misfortune did not happen just to me and my family. Millions of people and families have been devastated. . . . Why I do not want to speak about Partition? The reason is that the murderers could not be caught, nor were they punished. People who killed and looted were strangers. No one could have recognized them. When you do not know the murderers, why this complaint or lamentation?' Cf. the remarks of a Hebrew writer who survived the Nazi concentration camps: 'After liberation the one desire was to sleep, to forget and to be reborn. At first there was a wish to talk incessantly about one's experiences; this gave way to silence, but learning to be silent was not easy. When the past was no longer talked about, it became unreal, a figment of one's imagination.' Aharon Appelfeld, quoted in Martin S. Bergmann and Milton E. Jucovy (eds), *Generations of the Holocaust* (New York: Columbia University Press, 1982, pp. 5–6).

you will understand? Today your world is very different from mine.'[14] But he also adds, 'If you want to talk, why don't you talk about the thieves who have been in power since 1947? . . . this Rajiv, this Indira and this Nehru . . . all of them talked about independence. But did they ever mention Partition and the suffering. For them we were just refugees.'[15] The survivor goes on to say:

Honestly, when the experience was raw, I never felt like talking to my children about Partition. The children were too young to understand. When they grew up, so many other things kept coming up. . . . It is not that I have not discussed it with others, but they had similar experiences; so they understood. In itself Partition was bitter, but the treatment meted out to us by the Delhiwallas was worse. The word 'refugee' has stuck to us; the local people usually do not marry us. It is true that before 1947 even we—the West Punjabis—never thought of marrying people from this side. Even now, they have a certain attitude towards refugees. Often I think that we could have stayed back and given a tough fight instead of fleeing like *Bhagoras* [cowards].[16]

There are other reasons, too, which are slowly surfacing. Many of the killers are now in their late seventies or eighties. They are venerable grandparents and village elders. For years some of them did not talk about Partition, perhaps partly out of vague fears over legal consequences and social approbation. Others were torn because they had killed, or actively participated in the self-immolation of members of their own families and community. Chaudhuri Mangal Ram claims that he was young and hot-blooded in 1947. As he could not cross the newly created border to avenge the death of Hindus in Pakistan, he had to console himself by killing a few innocent Muslims nearer home. The Hindus of

[14] Meenakshi Verma, Interview with Ram Narain, a refugee who was a spare-parts dealer at Bhawalpur, Pakistan, in August 1997 at Delhi.

[15] Verma, Interview with Ram Narain.

[16] Verma, Interview with Ram Narain.

Pakistan were also innocent, he ventures as an excuse. He hastens to add, however, that he is now old and a different person; he would not now opt for the same concept of revenge.[17] Captain Nihal Singh of Rohtak, afraid that he might not able to protect his wife, in an advanced state of pregnancy in 1947, shot her dead and has reportedly never been the same again.

Such people are now less afraid; they have made some sort of peace with their past. This was not so even a few years ago. The case of fifty-three-year-old Jeet Behn, from a large family of Sikhs in Dheri, near Rawalpindi, is not atypical. She provides an example of memories that resist exposure.

A Muslim friend offered shelter to all 21 of us. . . . Our Muslim host barricaded the door of the room with grain bags. The mob returned next morning. . . . They jeered, yelled that if we came out, ate halal meat, converted to Islam, we'd be spared. Father refused, yelling back we'd prefer to die.

. . . Father handed each of us kirpans [small ritual swords] explaining carefully that if the mob broke the door we should stab ourselves on the *left* side. My mother, nursing my three-month old brother, threw herself at father's feet saying, 'Save this child. Agree to convert.' Father ignored her. When she repeated her entreaty my elder uncle got up, slashed her neck with a kirpan yelling, *yeh kehna haraam hai* [This is blasphemy]. She died instantly. Father put her blood-soaked *dupatta* on the tip of his sword, rushed out of the door half-crazed. People waiting on the other side literally skewered him with knives and swords. My eldest uncle who rushed out after him was similarly cut down. The doctor cousin got up to fight next. His wife stopped him, demanding he kill her, all the girls, before he went out. He stabbed her, killed his three-year-old son, stabbed each one of us. I still carry that kirpan scar on my scalp; and rushed out as we collapsed around him. He refused to stab his mother saying, 'No dharma tells me to do this.' He was lynched in seconds. Last to go was my octogenarian *daadi* [grandmother]. She tottered out, frail but resolute, saying, *Kaisi ladai ladney aaye ho? Mujhe apne bacchon ko ek baar dekhna hain.* [What kind of war is this? Let me at least see my

---

[17] Meenakshi Verma, Interview with Chaudhuri Mangal Ram, 1997.

children once.] They ripped out her earrings, bangles, gold chain. And as she stood there bleeding, stoned her to death. Before they left they slaughtered the Muslim bhai.[18]

Urvashi Butalia supplies even more gruesome instances of such self-destruction.[19] And the self-immolation of Sikh women in March 1947 in Thoa Khalsa village, Rawalpindi district, where nearly ninety of them jumped into a well to avoid dishonour, has become a legend. Such experiences, after a point, throttle speech. Many respondents can even now smell the rotting bodies of the victims. Others stutter when they try to remember those days.[20]

These passions, when remembered in tranquillity, do not encourage one to speak; they induce one to distance oneself from those times and be silent. Indeed, they invoke an 'encapsulated' self and stories about the self with which one cannot live comfortably in normal times.[21] On the basis of his conversations with Sikh participants in Partition violence, who live near the India–Pakistan border, Suketu Mehta describes the guilt-ridden silence that has come to be associated with memories of the carnage.[22] They also

[18] Jeet Behn, in Sunil Mehra and Prashant Pajiar (with Azhar Abbas, Mazhar Zaidi, Arshad Mahmood, Soutik Biswas and Pritha Sen), 'Sufferers and Survivors', *Outlook*, 28 May 1997, p. 32–51; see esp. p. 51.

[19] Urvashi Butalia, 'Community, State and Gender: On Women's Agency During Partition', *Economic and Political Weekly*, 24 April 1993, pp. WS-12–22.

[20] Though survival in some cases did depend on being silent during the Partition riots, there was nothing corresponding to the silence enforced through violence and executions in the concentration camps: 'Crying or making a face when one was hit in a concentration camp was a crime that would prompt immediate execution. The conspiracy of silence in survivors, persecutors, and their children has many determinants; but, no doubt, it also has as its source the taboo on telling and denial instituted by the Nazis themselves and continued to this day by the neo-Nazis.' Judhth S. Kestenberg, 'Introduction', Part III: The Persecutors' Children, in Bergmann and Jucovy, *Generations of the Holocaust*, pp. 161–6; see esp. p. 162.

[21] Cf. Henry Abramowitz, 'There are No Words: Two Greek–Jewish Survivors of Auschwitz', *Analytic Psychology*, 1986, 3(3), pp. 201–16.

[22] Mehta, 'Partition'.

encourage one to think of those times as essentially sinful, not worth remembering. 'I shall tell you what is *pap, gandagi* . . . when a man lusts for another man's blood, and that too without any personal animosity, when a man has a woman at home and yet defiles helpless other women. Don't you think that is *pap* [sin]?'[23]

Among our informants, one couple, married for forty years, have never discussed the Partition violence between them, though both lost their fathers in the violence. Some other survivors have taken the silence to its logical conclusion; they show signs of mutism and dissociative reactions. Still others entered acute anxiety states during the interviews. One became incoherent while describing his experiences; he had wandered around in Pakistan for months after Partition, self-oblivious and probably in a state of dissociation till an army convoy noticed his name tattooed on his forearm in Gurmukhi and sent him to India.[24] Another respondent, even after fifty years, choked every time he tried to say something about his experiences.[25]

Probably the last word on that silence has been said by Gulzar, the writer and film director, in his story *Raavi Paar*, recently translated into English.[26] It borrows, I am told, from an older, central Indian story that pre-dates the Partition. In Gulzar's version, it is the story of a couple running away with two children, who are twins, in a train from West Pakistan to a city in India. One of the children is already dead but the mother will not part with the body. On the advice of his fellow passengers, the concerned father at one point picks ups what he thinks is the body of the dead child and throws it out of the train into the river Raavi while his

[23] Meenakshi Verma, Interview with Rajendra Kaur, formerly of Rawalpindi, now at Delhi, August 1997.

[24] Meenakshi Verma, Interview with Darshan Kakkar, Delhi, January 1997.

[25] Meenakshi Verma, Interview with Suchcha Shah, Chandigarh, September 1997.

[26] Gulzar, 'Raavi Paar', trans. Alok Bhalla, in *Raavi Paar and Other Stories* (New Delhi: HarperCollins, 1997), pp. 42–7.

wife sleeps with the other child. The scream of the child thrown away tells him it was the wrong child. The child who reached safety is dead; it cannot speak. The living child, who could have spoken, has been lost on the way or left behind.

Given the magnitude of the killings, the fate of those who were merely uprooted has attracted even less scholarly attention. Except for a rewritten doctoral dissertation by Steven Keller, there is almost nothing systematic on the subject.[27] Yet sixteen million is a large number, even in South Asia. They, together with the one million dead, have found ways of insidiously entering South Asia's political agenda. The public cultures of Pakistan, the whole of north India, Bangladesh, and to a lesser extent east and west India—especially the cities—have never been the same again. They bear the unmistakable stamp of that insidious entry.

My aim here is not to record the memories of victims in order to construct narratives for the historian in a cultural region that mostly does not live by history. It is to identify the way in which South Asians grapple with their trauma, by selectively owning up or disowning their memories, or by reconfiguring them. These then survive in private and shared fantasies, influencing the public life of the region, often without anyone being the wiser.

III

COMPARING GENOCIDES

The European holocaust, the most thoroughly studied genocide of all times, had a number of unique features which distinguished it from other genocides and pogroms directed against European Jewish communities in earlier times. Two of these features have

---

[27] Stephen Keller, *Uprooting and Social Change: The Role of Refugees in Development* (Delhi: Manohar, 1975).

been repeatedly emphasized and debated in recent works because of their relevance to our times. Firstly, not only did the state collude—as many states had earlier—with the genocide and pogroms, it systematically built a mega-machine for the final solution. A huge majority of Germans might have supported the killing of Jews, as Daniel Goldhagen's recent study insists,[28] but that support by itself would not have been enough. 'Genocide requires well-educated professionals. They are necessary for its technology, its organization, and its rationale. In the Nazi case, members of all the professions—physicians, scientists, engineers, military leaders, lawyers, clergy, university professors, and school teachers—were effectively mobilized to the ideological project.'[29] Second, nineteenth-century science, especially biology and specifically eugenics, has been increasingly identified as the principal source of the legitimacy built for ethnic cleansing in Germany. As with some of its pocket editions—the nuclear bombing of Hiroshima and Nagasaki and the fire bombing of Dresden and Tokyo—the Jewish holocaust was more a pathology of human rationality than of irrationality.[30] Even the Stalinist terror, which killed an estimated two million, derived sanction from scientized history serving as

[28] Daniel Jonah Goldhagen, *Hitler's Willing Executioners: Ordinary Germans and the Holocaust* (New York: Knopf, 1996). For a critique of Goldhagen from a point of view not incompatible with that of this paper, see C. Fred Alford, 'Hitler's Willing Executioners: What Does "Willing" Mean', *Theory and Society*, October 1997, 26(5), pp. 719–38. For an excellent, systematic, empirical assessment of this issue, see A.D. Moses, 'Structure and Agency in the Holocaust: Daniel J. Goldhagen and His Critics', *History and Theory*, 1998, 37(2), pp. 194–219.

[29] Robert J. Lifton and Erik Markusen, *The Genocidal Mentality: Nazi Holocaust and Nuclear Threat* (New York: Basic Books, 1990), p. 98.

[30] This issue has been empirically explored in Robert J. Lifton, *Nazi Doctors: Medical Killing and the Psychology of Genocide* (New York: Basic Books, 1986). The classic statement of this position is of course Hannah Arendt, *Eichmann in Jerusalem* (Harmondsworth: Penguin, 1965); for a more recent exploration, see Zigmunt Bauman, *Modernity and the Holocaust* (Ithaca: Cornell University, 1991).

another form of evolutionism. In retrospect it seems that, if not the root, certainly the ultimate justification of the holocaust was a concept of knowledge and social engineering that had come to dominate European consciousness. The German attitude to the victims of the final solution was not particularly different from that of a farmer's towards a heap of dead insects after the pest controller has done his job.[31] Nothing reveals that attitude better than the chilling display at the Beit Hashoah Museum of Tolerance, Los Angeles, of the small artefacts that were to constitute parts of a projected Museum of an Extinct Race. The Nazis planned to set up the museum after they had finally 'solved' the Jewish problem. The authorities of the Los Angeles museum seem unaware that the project was perfectly compatible with a significant part of the European record in the tropics during the last three hundred years.

Perhaps as a result, while there was resistance to the violence and the totalism of the European holocaust, that resistance was infrequent, unorganized, scattered and usually individual. The inadequate resistance among the Jews, problematized in the 1940s by the likes of Bruno Bettelheim,[32] is well known. However, there has been no comparable interest in the infrequent resistance among Germans to the genocide of Jews. Its infrequency has indirectly fuelled recent works such as Goldhagen's.

The compulsive form which the search for ethnic purity took in the Nazi millennial ideology was also directly legitimized by the nineteenth-century idea of public hygiene. Race was very nearly a sexually transmitted disease. Even young Germans planning to marry had, under the Nazi racial laws, to declare under oath that

[31] The inner logic of this attitude found its final expression in the Cambodian holocaust. In that carnage, one-third of a country was liquidated for the benefit of the remaining two-thirds, strictly according to the principles of scientific history as taught by some respectable academics within the portals of the Sorbonne to eager students who later served as ideologues of the genocide in Cambodia.

[32] Bruno Bettelheim, *Surviving and Other Essays* (New York: Alfred A. Knopf, 1979).

their parents and grandparents were not Jewish. The fear of racial contamination was a bizarre and comical part of German cultural and intellectual life during the 1930s. Together, these two features ensured that not only were the victims of the holocaust denied human status, there was a cultivated dehumanization of the perpetrators and those who served as cogs in the wheel of the machine built for the genocide of Jews, gypsies and other such groups in Europe. The ideas of dispassionate, rational statecraft and objective, value-neutral knowledge, pushed to their limits, almost automatically led to Auschwitz, Belsen, Treblinka and Dachau.

Both the features—the industrialization of mass murder and the search for its sanction in Baconian rationality and modern biology—were marginal to Partition violence. The attempt to obliterate the other community frequently went hand in hand with attempts to forcibly convert enemies to one's own faith. It is a different matter that two of the main communities involved, Sikhs and Punjabi Muslims, were so close to each other that they had lived in perpetual, mortal fear of losing their identities. Conversion, even when fake or superficial, looked to them worse than death; they often chose death rather than conversion. A large proportion of the abducted women too were not raped and abandoned, nor used as sex slaves. The abductors and/or rapists often ended up by marrying them and integrating them in their community. There are accounts of how, when some of these women were later identified and, consistent with their rights as citizens, repatriated to the 'right' countries according to their faiths, many of their abductors-turned-husbands broke down and stood for days at the borders trying to get a glimpse of their 'victims', and the victims themselves 'resisted their lives being disrupted again by the "state" recovering them.'[33] Admitting these bonds is not an attempt to deny the violence, humiliation and gender injustice in the situation. It is to

---

[33] Khan, 'Identity, Violence and Women', p. 165. For excellent detailed work in this area, see Veena Das, *Critical Events: An Anthropological Perspective on Contemporary India* (New Delhi: Oxford University Press, 1995), ch. 3.

acknowledge that, at a time when pathological forms of thinking and emotions abounded, at least there was no paranoid search for racial and ethnic purity that characterized the genocidal mentality in the Third Reich. Nor was the killing of the enemy ever turned into an industry or a dispassionate, official duty.[34]

On such grounds, some may refuse to classify the violence of 1946–8 among even the major Asian genocides of our times, such as the Armenian and Cambodian ones. Partition violence began as small, organized skirmishes that escalated into major bloodbaths, often helped by blatantly partisan police and state officials. But the armies were on the whole not involved (though retired army men, in some instances, were) and the infant states of India and Pakistan were complicit more by their inactivity than via active intervention. Perhaps the most distinctive feature of the violence in South Asia was that all the victims knew that in other parts of the region, often only a few miles away, people from their own community were doing exactly what was being done to them. As a result, some who were victims of torture or had even lost their entire families retained their moral balance. Even Jeet Behn, the victim from Rawalpindi whom we have met earlier, says, 'Do I feel any rage? No. *Maahaul bura tha. Log bure nahin the. Wo waqt hi bure the.*' [The atmosphere was bad. People weren't evil. The times themselves were bad.][35]

That is probably why the violence has not divided the three communities permanently into victims (constantly asking themselves why they could be slaughtered so easily) and oppressors (constantly asking themselves how they could turn killers so effortlessly), both looking to the past with a mixture of guilt and defensiveness. Each major community in South Asia feels that it

[34] Veena Das and Ashis Nandy, 'Violence, Victimhood and the Language of Silence', in Veena Das (ed.), *The Word and the World: Fantasy, Symbol and Record* (New Delhi: Sage, 1986), pp. 177–96.

[35] Jeet Behn, in Mehra and Pajiar, 'Sufferers and Survivors', p. 51.

was cheated by the Partition and more victimized in the riots, but knows that the other also suffered and feels aggrieved. There are also people in each community who paradoxically feel that their community won the battle, for it had inflicted greater and 'purer' suffering on the others.[36] 'Whosoever from the Hindus and Sikhs came in front of us, were killed. Not only that, we got them to come out of their houses and ruthlessly killed them and disgraced their womenfolk. Many women agreed to come with us and wished us to take them, but we were out for revenge.'[37]

Through this wall of pain, fear, hatred, and silence some have at long last begun to look at the birth trauma of India and Pakistan. One of the earliest to work on the subject, Nighat Said Khan speaks on behalf of her collaborator, Anis Haroon, and herself: 'We were aware that we ourselves, as children of Urdu-speaking migrants, and children of Pakistan, had never come to terms with the trauma of Partition; not because we come from homes that constantly and consciously lived in the past but because we had internalized an ongoing, if silent pain, and had never exorcised the horror not just of the violence, but of being a part of truncated identity.[38] The hope is that, as with journeys through madness, this journey of exploration too might turn out to be a step towards an alternative, enriched form of sanity, provided one knows how to work through the memories of the journey. Even chronicling the suffering of the survivor, to ensure that cold statistics do not hide the reality of the suffering, can be therapeutic. For it opens up the culture of politics to unconditional empathy and the courage to admit that the recognition of suffering must have priority

[36] There is, however, a feeling in some sections of the Hindus that they did not match the aggression of the two 'martial' communities in the conflict, the Muslims and the Sikhs. See B.L. Sharma Prem on this subject later.

[37] Letter to a relative from a subaltern in the Punjab Regiment, quoted in Gyanendra Pandey, 'Partition, History and the Making of Nations' (Delhi: Department of History, Delhi University, 1995), unpublished ms., p. 10.

[38] Khan, 'Identity, Violence and Women', p. 167.

over the celebration of fictitious entities such as nation-states and nationalism in South Asia.

What about other instances of ethnic or religious violence in South Asia? After all, communal or religious riots were not unknown in British India. Were the Partition riots in continuity with them and with the communal riots that have since become routine in parts of South Asia?

It is doubtful. First, one identifiable feature of present-day religious and ethnic violence in South Asia is the diminishing component of passion. Most organizers and participants in such riots are professional or semi-professional small-time politicians who deem it part of their job to occasionally provoke or organize collective violence. There are sections in many metropolitan slums that get itchy if no riot takes place for a while. A riot means to them easy access to money and pillaged consumables. It is also a criminal activity for which there is temporary moral sanction, even if it is partial and comes from only a section of the people. These activist–rioters are quite ecumenical. When not engaged in communal violence, they participate in caste riots, extortion rackets and election rigging. Well paid by South Asian standards and well protected politically, they are not spread among different communities randomly. Communities suffering social discrimination are usually better represented in such extra-social groups, for crime— like the entertainment industry, politics, the stock market, and spectator sports—is often a more open system than the more established industries and professions. Also, serious organizers of collective violence tend to maintain excellent relations with others of their ilk on the wrong side of religious, caste and ideological

[39] On the dominant political culture of communal violence, see Ashis Nandy, 'The Politics of Secularism; Recovery of Religious Tolerance', *Alternatives*, 1988, 13(3), and 'The Twilight of Certitudes', *Alternatives*, 1997, 22(1), pp. 177–94.

boundaries.[39] They are professionals and are not entirely taken in by their own language of hate.

This professional status and the absence of malice is recognized by society, and certainly by the political class. It may not be outrageous to claim that not a single major rioter or riot organizer during the last fifty years has gone to jail in any of the four major countries of South Asia that have seen religious or sectarian violence. The late C.V. Subba Rao, a human rights activist who had researched communal violence for years, once said that the official commission that enquired into the fierce riots at Bhiwandi near Bombay during 1992–3 found ten policemen guilty of complicity with the rioters and imposed on them fines of Rs 10 each, payable in instalments.[40]

In 1946–8, on the other hand, riots had a more impassioned quality about them and, at places, they *did* involve a degree of fervour, even religious fervour. Those active in the riots *did* feel that they had to take on the responsibility of defending their kind and teach their enemies a lesson, perhaps the last series of riots in which a majority of the participants might have thought thus. The Partition riots were probably the closest to being large-scale religious riots in the last fifty years in South Asia.

Second, Partition violence was not merely the murder and pillage of others; it also involved massive violence directed towards the self. The mass suicide at Thoa Khalsa was not an isolated instance; 'stories of this kind of mass suicide, or of women being killed by their own families, are legion', Butalia says.[41] We shall not deal here with the important questions Butalia raises in this connection, but one should note that, to sharpen her critique of patriarchy, Butalia underscores the fear of dishonour as the cause

[40] C.V. Subba Rao, Seminar on the Profile of Communal Violence in India, at the Centre for the Study of Developing Societies, October 1995.

[41] Butalia, 'Community, State and Gender'. In the non-fictional writings on Partition that have emanated from India's modern sector, Butalia is one of the few who have paid serious attention to this part of the story.

of suicide. The data she uses herself show that just as important was the fear of losing one's religion and culture.[42] That other fear seems to enjoy little respect in Butalia's secularized world.

Third, though only one-fourth of Indians stay in cities, roughly two-third of all communal riots in India today takes place in cities. If one goes by origin, probably no less than 95 per cent of riots in India originate in its cities. In the last fifty years only 3.6 per cent of the victims of religious violence have died in the villages, even though roughly 80 per cent of Indians have lived in villages during the period.[43] Religious violence in India—presumably in the whole of South Asia—has a clear urban connection.

Here too the violence of 1946–8 was different. It spread to villages in the whole of Punjab and in large pockets of East Bengal and Bihar. It is true that detailed studies have begun to show that the whole of northern India was not in flames, as many have believed for years. They also show that there were elements of planning and organization in the riots too; that they were not all

[42] Among the survivors who escaped to India almost all the cases of such mass suicide involved Sikhs. And Khan in 'Identity, Violence and Women' mentions similar instances of self-destruction among Muslims escaping India. This may have something to do with the complex, close relationship and intertwined self-definitions of Sikhs and Muslims in the Punjab. These intertwined self-definitions often go with extreme fears of losing identity. There are clues to this complex relationship in J.P. Uberoi, *Religion, Civil Society and the State: A Study of Sikhism* (Delhi: Oxford University Press, 1996). Also relevant to this issue is Stanley J. Tambiah, 'Obliterating the "Other" in Former Yugoslavia', *Nethra*, January–March 1997, 1(2), pp. 7–35. The same issue emerges in other forms in Gananath Obeyesekere, 'Dutthagamani and the Buddhist Conscience', in Douglas Allen (ed.), *Religion and Political Conflict in South Asia* (New Delhi: Oxford University Press, 1993), pp. 135–60; and Vamik D. Volkan, *The Need to Have Enemies and Allies* (New York: Jason Aronson, 1988). We shall return to this subject.

[43] Ashis Nandy, 'Coping with the Politics of Faiths and Cultures: Between Secular State and Ecumenical Traditions in India', Darini Rajasingham-Senanayake, Ashis Nandy and Edmund T. Gomez, *Ethnic Futures: The State and Identity Politics in Asia* (New Delhi: Sage, 1999), pp. 135–66; Ashutosh Varshney, 'Civic Life and Ethnic Conflict', unpublished ms.

spontaneity and fanaticism.[44] But it is also becoming clearer that the riots were not merely a speciality of the cities or a matter of urban slums exploding in violence. South Asian society, including rural South Asia, *was* implicated in the Partition riots.

Fourth, unlike most recent riots in South Asia, the Partition riots were not one-sided. They were one-sided only at any one point of time and space; otherwise each community knew that in other parts of the region there were others avenging its suffering and humiliation. Some not merely knew this but also saw what such revenge meant:

Shahid Ahmed's train journey ended in Lahore where, he recounts, sections of the waiting crowd proceeded at once to determine whether the train had been attacked and how many had been killed or wounded. They then promised summary justice. 'Wait!', they said, according to Shahid Ahmed, 'we shall settle scores right now, in your presence': and, stopping a refugee special going the other way at Baghbanpura station just outside Lahore, they paid back the killers of Eastern Punjab in their own coin—'with interest'.[45]

This element of 'balance' did not mitigate the suffering, but allowed many victims to retain their sensitivity to the nature of the violence. There was another additional element of 'equity': sizeable sections in each community continued to believe that their community was the wronged party in 1946–8, victimized and denied justice by those who ganged up against it.

IV

ACCOUNTABILITY AND RESISTANCE

History lies not by misrepresenting reality but by exiling emotions. Memories, and the myths that enshrine them, stand witness by refusing to discard human subjectivity. Myths are not

---

[44] For instance, Shail Mayaram, *Resisting Regimes: Memory and the Shaping of a Muslim Identity* (New Delhi: Oxford University Press, 1997).

[45] Pandey, 'Partition and Independence', p. 2271.

people's history or alternative history, their job is to resist history and resist the objectification of suffering and sufferers in the name of objectivity. Thus, the memories of Partition often have little to do with the known reality or scale of riots. Many Sindhi refugees, for instance, are traumatized not by the direct experience of violence but by the loss of their ancestral home and the debilitating fear of losing one's culture and identity in a new setting. Often they cannot articulate this fear, for the culture they are afraid of losing is the one they shared with their Muslim neighbours. That culture included not only a shared past, landscape, and language, but also places of worship and concepts of the divine. Their anguish may seem disproportionate to their loss to us, but to some of them the low level of anguish in younger Sindhis at the loss of their culture is itself a matter of serious concern.

Victims organize their memories in diverse ways, in response to their own inner needs, but the diversity is not random or infinite because the needs are not so. Some patterns dominate. First, there are the sophisticated, articulate respondents supplying highly intellectualized, quasi-academic, socio-economic interpretations of their suffering. At the time of independence, there were areas in South Asia where religious differences coincided with deep divisions of caste, class and vocation. It does not require much perspicacity or moral courage to own up that, in some of these areas, the cumulative rage of the oppressed—at being subjected to economic hardships, social discrimination and humiliation—spoke through communal riots.

For instance, some victims who belonged to the erstwhile Hindu élite of East Bengal readily admit that the brutal exploitation and discrimination experienced by the Muslim peasantry found an outlet in anti-Hindu violence in 1946–8. In Noakhali in East Bengal, Gandhi's personal secretary Nirmal Kumar Bose— in his other incarnation a distinguished cultural anthropologist— surveyed the pattern of landholding in the district. Bose found that while Hindus were 18 per cent of the population, they owned three-fourths of the land. Muslims, who constituted 82 per cent of the population, were mostly peasants, directly confronting the disparity in their everyday life and living in dire poverty.[46] Yet Noakhali was a district noted for Islamic activism and fervour. The mix turned out to be volatile. To an extent, the reverse was the case in some pockets of Bihar where, too, the carnage in 1946–7 was fearsome. The victims who mention socio-economic discrimination as the major source of Partition violence, and ultimately of their own dislocation and suffering, may not have direct access to such data, but they somehow sensed, often as children, the bitterness that was gradually building up. Hindsight may have sharpened their convictions.

Second, some victims remember their suffering as an act of fate or destiny. They cannot otherwise explain how, even in places where different religious communities that had lived together in reasonable amity for centuries, inter-communal relations suddenly snapped. To these victims, Partition violence was something like a natural calamity—a cyclone, plague or a holocaust in its older sense of *pralaya*—that had befallen the country at the time. One Hindu refugee describes how his community, an isolated one living at the margins of near-desert conditions, instead of moving towards India, moved deeper into the wilderness. Some Shia communities of the area joined it once they heard of the violence all around.[47] Apparently, these communities wanted to avoid what they saw as a strange abnormality spreading from the cities, not as a standard inter-religious feud.

Many such victims are not angry with the enemy community for being cruel or homicidal. They believe that for a brief

[46] Nirmal Kumar Bose, *My Days with Gandhi* (Calcutta: Nishana, 1953), p. 33.

[47] Meenakshi Verma, Interview with Sukhvinder Nijhawan, Chandigarh, September 1997.

while, in parts of north India, humanity itself collapsed.[48] Their exposure to the dishonesty and betrayal by some members of their own community has confirmed this belief. They have not forgotten that their own relatives and friends sometimes took advantage of those chaotic times to cheat or pauperize them. A few victims offset the help they received from friends in the 'enemy community' against the way their own relatives, who sheltered them as refugees, quickly got tired of them.[49] In a couple of cases, these respondents have described how, even when family friends or distant relatives abducted or ran away with a woman in the family, the family had to publicly claim that someone from the enemy community had done this. In those troubled times, it was not only believable but had become an accepted way of protecting family honour. At least one respondent claims that her husband, in a drunken rage, killed their two children by throwing them off their terrace at Lahore and then blamed Muslims for killing them.

Third, many survivors remember how, even in those bitter days, when inter-community relations were at their nadir, individuals and communities resisted the violence. Many neighbours did succumb to greed and the temptation to loot, but others risked their lives—and that of their families—to protect friends and even strangers from the other community. A few even died trying to protect their wards.[50] A large number of the

[48] Meenakshi Verma, Interview with Kalawati Verma, Delhi, March 1997; Dulari Nagpal, Delhi, April 1997; Jaspreet Kaur, Delhi, April 1997; Kantarani Dhingra, Delhi, May 1997; Lado Talwar, Chandigarh, September 1997.

[49] For instance, Jagdish Prakash, 'End of Innocence', in 'Train From Pakistan', *The Pioneer*, 26 January 1997.

[50] The concept of survivor as used in this section has a particular slant. While it carries the meaning associated with it in such pioneering works on genocide as that of Robert J. Lifton, it also means in the South Asian context someone who has faced genocidal violence but has also experienced some help from someone in the enemy community, a help that has not merely ensured his or her survival but has also become permanently intertwined with the memory of that violence. A survivor is a witness to both human depravity and human potentialities.

survivors have at least one story to tell about how a member of the 'enemy community' helped them or saved their lives. One of them, a Hindu refugee from what is now Bangladesh, remembers:

My sister-in-law was heavily pregnant, and the tension suddenly brought on the labour pains. There was no shelter, but finally there was an upper class Muslim family who welcomed them in. The . . . people were still the same; it was just that terror suddenly spread. . . . They told my sister-in-law, 'Mother, do not mind, but you have to take off the white bangles [*shakha*] from your wrists, and somehow manage to take off the *sindoor* from the parting of your hair [the signs of a married Bengali Hindu woman]. She was then dressed in the dress and anklets [*paijeb*] of the daughter-in-law of the house. . . . Her hair was rearranged too—she was made into a member of the family without hesitation. She delivered a male child under these circumstances.[51]

There is no biographical or psychological data available till now on the rescuers who defied the atmosphere of hate in 1946–8. One can only speculate about the culture and early developmental experiences that facilitated their moral integrity. Most of them fell— one guesses from the narratives of the victims—in categories that Eva Fogelman identifies as religious–moral and emotional–moral rescuers.[52] It is, however, obvious that such individuals were far more numerous in South Asia. Those who resisted in Germany shared some common traits, the most important being deep religious faith, intact community ties, and positive experiences and memories of childhood. It could be that, in the matter of religious beliefs and community ties at least, South Asian cultures were more fortunate.

Survivors do not all like to remember these moments of generosity. After recounting such episodes, some quickly explain away

[51] Anindita Mukhopadhyaya, 'The Humane Face', *The Hindu*, 31 August 1997.

[52] Eva Fogelman, 'Victims, Perpetrators, Bystanders, and Rescuers in the Face of Genocide and Its Aftermath . . .' in Charles B. Strozier and Michael Flynn (eds), *Genocide, War and Human Survival* (New York: Rowman and Littlefield, 1996), pp. 87–98; see pp. 91–2.

the generosity as an exception that should not be over-emphasized or blown out of proportion. As in other parts of the world, the victims of collective violence in 1946–8 supply a steady stream of easy recruits to fundamentalist and ultra-nationalist politics; they want to make sure that their memories do not cramp their contemporary politics. Defensively, they provide elaborate explanations of why neighbourly gestures by people from another faith must not negate the community stereotypes they have chosen to live with. In addition, thanks to the sensitivities promoted by studies of genocide—many of them done from within a quasi-Freudian framework—there is nowadays a premium on cynicism and a tough-minded interpretation of occasional neighbourliness. At the ground level, such cynicism and tough-mindedness can even be seen as a cover for deeper hatred, jealousy, and greed—a posture compatible with fundamentalist and ultra-nationalist constructions of the past.

Kirpal Raj is a case in point. He does not remember his date of birth but knows that he was about twelve years old at the time of Partition. After he came to India, he was admitted to a middle school at Sonepat in 1948 by an RSS worker. This worker had looked after him and borne his educational and other expenses since he was brought to Amritsar by the Indian army. Raj feels beholden to this man, a practitioner of traditional medicine. This influences his remembrance of things past.

Young Kirpal's journey began suddenly, without any warning. One day, he went to the fields to relieve himself around twilight and decided to wander till the late hours as he was afraid of being beaten by his father. Suddenly he heard cheerful cries of *Allah ho Akbar*, the meaning of which, at the time, was not clear to him. He decided to stay back. The evening took a macabre turn when, while standing among the tall sugarcane stalks, he saw a young man running. Kirpal asked him why he was running so breathlessly.

The stranger pointed towards the village and said, 'Don't go back; they are killing people. They will kill everyone.'

Whenever I have tried to recall and talk about my parents and my brothers, the images that crowd my memory are fire balls leaping high up in the air and very incoherent and mixed cries of various types. The cattle wailed the loudest, especially the buffaloes; this is the strongest memory I have of that evening. . . .

. . . It had rained heavily, I felt cold and after few hours, I started shivering . . . then I just fell on the muddy ground. . . . After that what I remember is that I was in a bed with people around me.

He recognized the people around him; they belonged to a Muslim family that lived nearby. The head of the family was Rahmat Mian and his wife was Kariman, whom Kirpal knew. Their sons were his friends; their daughter Mehrunissa he used to tease as Mehru. Kirpal guesses that the family discovered him in the field and brought him home. He was not told that his family had been killed along with other non-Muslim villagers.

Kirpal was delirious with fever for a few days. He gathered later that he had typhoid. When he asked about his family, he was told they had gone elsewhere and would return later. 'One day one of the boys told me that my parents were dead and so were my four brothers. And so were my grandmother, grandfather, and great grandmother.'[53] Raj guesses that he was the only Hindu who survived. One day he asked Kariman Bee if it was true that the others had been killed. She did not answer. It was again one of their sons who said yes, all the Hindus and Sardars [Sikhs] were killed, and they were burnt too. Raj felt acutely uneasy. Later, Rahmat Mian took him to the nearest camp. Raj does not feel obliged to Rahmat's family at all:

I have not felt obliged towards the Muslim family which saved me because. . . . I think had I not hidden in the fields even I too would have

[53] Meenakshi Verma, Interview with Kirpal Raj, Delhi, June, 1997.

been killed . . . what happened to the Muslim neighbours who did not come to rescue their non-Muslim neighbours when they were being killed. . . . Not rescuing was also a form of participation in killing. How did it matter to them if a kid lived or died. . . . We had known these people for generations?[54]

Fourth, some victims organize their memories around instances of 'strange', culturally imposed limits to violence that surprised them in those amoral times. In one case, some Pathans attacked a Sikh village and offered to spare all if they converted to Islam. The Sikhs being Sikhs, turned down the offer. The Pathans killed all the men of the village but escorted some 200 women and children to a camp set up for refugees. The interviewee who lost her father, uncle, and two brothers says: 'Pathans are very honest . . . they will never touch things which do not belong to them.'[55] She also indicates that their experience could not even be shared with others, for no one would have believed at the time that they were spared by Muslims at a time when hundreds of thousands of women had been raped and abducted by both sides.[56]

Less bizarre were efforts to bind anxiety through black humour. Though it perhaps did not turn violence and death into laughter, even metaphorically such humour did probably lessen the guilt that people felt on behalf of—or in identifying with—their own communities.[57] The following instance is from what is now Bangladesh:

Suja Khalid had recognized the probable consequence of the political turbulence and communal violence on the life of his Hindu friend—his eventual departure from East Bengal. He requested [Prasanna] Sen to

[54] Ibid.

[55] Meenakshi Verma, 'The Survivor's Story', *The Hindu*, 24 August 1997.

[56] Ibid.

[57] Anindita Mukhopadhyaya, 'The Last Journey', *The Hindu*, 31 August 1997.

pay a visit to his ancestral home in the village. Perhaps for the last time. Yet he phrased the request in the form of light banter. 'I have got it; you are going to run off, too! This time I am not going to let you off—you will have to come to our village.'

Prasanna immediately understood the hidden message and he answered in the same vein: 'You will finish me off if I come with you!' . . . Suja shot back, 'If you die at the hands of a friend, you will go to heaven and, if you die in the hands of a stranger, you will go to hell.'[58]

No wonder Sen, when describing his last journey across the border, expresses in no uncertain terms his pride in his uncle's decision to stay back at the request of the Muslim inhabitants of his village.

Finally, there is a small group of people who have come to hate their own communities for not hitting back strongly enough. B.L. Sharma Prem, an activist of the Rashtriya Swayam Sevak Sangh (RSS) since the age of eighteen and a Partition victim who used to live at Lahore, is a colourful, if venomous instance:

Hindu resistance *theek maatra mein nahin hui* [wasn't equivalent]. Hindus were more interested in looting rather than killing. Hindu women produce rats. Not fighters. That's why we lost our self-respect, our women, our *izzat*, Punjab, Sindh, Kashmir to the Muslims in 1947. . . . I tell you in hardly 10 years India will be a Muslim country. Muslim men are seducing Hindu women, reducing us to a minority. They know how to seduce: with kohl, bangles, dupattas. Their diet is *uttejak* [aphrodisiac]. Full of sex. Beef is full of sex. They mix it in liquor to feed their female victims. . . .

I'm a Parshurami pandit. Fundamentalist by birth, instinct, training. We believe politics must be Hinduized, Hindus must be militarized. *Yeh aag bujhne nahin deni* (we shouldn't let this fire die out). I only live for the day when the *tiranga* [the tricolour] will be unfurled on Pakistani territory. We should be like the Israelis. They greet each other with a 'Next year in Jerusalem'; we should say 'Next year in Lahore'.[59]

[58] Ibid.

[59] B.L. Sharma Prem, in Mehra and Pajiar, 'Sufferers and Survivors', pp. 38–9. Prem has recently, presumably out of disgust, converted to Sikhism.

Evidently, Sharma's Punjabi–Brahminic contempt for the non-martial, greedy Hindus—borrowed wholesale from Punjabi–Muslim and British colonial stereotypes—is matched only by his highly eroticized, jealous, angry fear of Muslims tinged with gender confusion and self-hatred.

Where does this impassioned hatred come from? One answer comes from studies drawing mainly upon the European holocaust. Another, with a different nuance, comes from scholars depending primarily on South Asian data. Stanley J. Tambiah sensitively captures that nuance when he spells out the 'diabolical riddle' in ethnic conflicts with an observation of George Simmel: 'The degeneration of a difference in convictions into hatred and fight occurs only when there were essential similarities between the parties. The "respect for the enemy" is usually absent where the hostility has arisen on the basis of previous solidarity.'[60] Tacitly invoking Freud's comment on the narcissism of small differences, Tambiah goes on to ask:

Can we push this process of creating and repudiating the intolerable 'other' in current ethnonationalist conflicts any further? Can we say that it is because that component of 'sameness' that the ethnic enemy shares with you, and because already your enemy is part of you, that you must forcibly expel him or her from yourself, objectify him or her as the *total other*? Accordingly, that component of 'difference from you, whether it be allegedly "religious" or "linguistic" or "racial" is so exaggerated and magnified that this stereotyped "other" must be degraded, dehumanized and compulsively *obliterated*.'[61]

The two answers are probably not mutually exclusive. For the South Asian experience might not be totally inapplicable to the case of the German Jews, without whom the self-definition of

[60] Stanley J. Tambiah, 'Obliterating the "Other" in Former Yugoslavia', pp. 7–8. Also Ashis Nandy, Shikha Trivedy, Achyut Yagnik and Shail Mayaram, *Creating a Nationality: The Ramjanmabhumi Movement and Fear of the Self* (New Delhi: Oxford University Press, 1995).

[61] Ibid.

modern Germans and the German culture could not—and perhaps still cannot—be complete in this century. 'Fear of loss of boundaries *is* the fear of loss of self, non-being.'[62] However, everyone who talks like Sharma need not necessarily have the record they themselves would prefer to have. One respondent claimed to have killed a number of Muslims and even gave details. Later, he abjectly admitted that they were all fictitious, designed to protect self-esteem and morale: 'We ourselves came to India as hungry nonentities that winter. How could we have killed any one?'[63]

V

THE VILLAGE IN AN ABRIDGED SELF

The journey of India, Pakistan, and Bangladesh as young nation-states cannot be narrated without reconstructing and working through the memories of the other journey that marked the death of the British empire in South Asia. Pandey seems to recognize this.[64] But the story of that other journey, in turn, cannot be told without mapping out the journey which the victims—and others identifying with them—have continued to make in their mind over the last five decades. That third journey, like a dirty unending war, has territorialized and frozen the shifting, fluid cultural and psychological borders among religious communities in South Asia. It is doubtful if the violence was a clash among existing nations, for the nineteenth-century European idea of nationality has never truly conveyed the distinctive South Asian forms of religious or cultural separateness. Indeed, the violence itself helped crystallize nation-like groupings with which

[62] Avner Falk, 'Border Symbolism Revisted', in Howard F. Stein and William G. Neiderland (eds), *Maps from the Mind: Reading Psychogeography* (London: University of Oklahoma, 1989), pp. 151–60 (p. 157).

[63] Meenakshi Verma, Interview with Aman Singh, Delhi, May 1997.

[64] Pandey, 'Partition, History and the Making of Nations'.

the ethnonationalists, the fundamentalists and even their modern secular foes, operating from various nineteenth-century European social-evolutionist positions, have gone to town. In South Asia at least, the new national boundaries are built not on the earlier distinctions, but on their ruins. To tell that part of the story, a word is required on that distinction and the plurality that has traditionally underpinned it.

South Asia has about 2,000 languages and dialects, of which at least 20 are spoken by more than a million people each. It has nearly 250,000 villages, 20,000 castes and endogamous subcastes, and virtually all the major religions of the world. Some of the religions not identified with the region—such as Christianity, Judaism, Islam, and Zoroastrianism—all have histories longer than a thousand years in the region. Two of them, Indian Christianity and Judaism, claim a history of two thousand years. Within its present boundaries, India includes more Muslims than any other country except Indonesia. Bangladesh, despite the massive exodus of Hindu population at the time of Partition and the continuous trickle of Hindus from it into India, is still the world's second largest Hindu country.

This diversity is organized not only territorially but also in intricate structures of interpenetrating, layered lifestyle, cultures, and self-definitions. According to a survey done in 1994 by the Anthropological Survey of India, about 425 communities in India have more than one religion.[65]

---

[65] K. Suresh Singh, *The People of India* (New Delhi: Oxford University Press, 1994), vol. 1. Such figures seem strange to only those unacquainted with Asian realities. Japanese census data tell us that in Japan the total number of people owing allegiance to different faiths exceeds the total population, mainly because many who claim to be Shinto also claim to be Buddhist. It might be fairly safe to presume that whatever kinds of violence Japan may suffer from, Shinto–   Buddhist strife will not be one of them. However, what seems a charming aberra-tion in Japan's case enjoys no status or legitimacy among the South Asian élite.

In a society organized more around culture than around politics, the survival of such communities was not difficult. But contemporary concepts of the nation-state and nationalism have not much place for them. The conventional ideas of citizenship and democracy have an enumerative thrust; they encourage the delineation of clear borders and well-defined selves. The culture that was a principal feature of social organization has been downsized as a baseline for political mobilization and competition for power in most of the region.

It is no surprise that, during the last one hundred years, no population census in India, Pakistan, Bangladesh, and Sri Lanka has identified a single person as belonging to more than one religion. If the survey led by K. Suresh Singh had not been done, such communities would have been seen only as anthropologist's delight or exotica. They would not have been considered relevant to larger issues of ethnic, religious, and sectarian violence in Indian society.

The Partition violence can be remembered in many ways—as an obscene instance of religious fanaticism, an aberration from Indian, specifically Gandhian, traditions of nonviolence and tolerance, or even as a fatal administrative failure (including the failure to gauge the dangerous possibilities that the division of British India opened up but need not have). I have bypassed these issues for the moment, concentrating instead on the way the memories of the period are structured today and the ways in which victims cope with them. A crucial element in this story is the way the ideas of the village and the city have been interwoven into the remembered past.

In this respect, there is a distinct trend in the imageries that we have unearthed. Many victims see the village as the source of evil and the explosion of rural violence as the ultimate proof of society coming unstuck. And they try hard to document that awareness. Jeet Behn says with the confidence of a statistician that 500 people from 15 villages participated in the second attack that killed her family, as if she had done a thorough survey.[66] Is she trying to say that the involvement of the villages was widespread, or that there was serious co-ordination and planning for the mob to have assembled from so many villages? We do not know. We can only surmise that this fear of villages, contaminated by an unknown poison that divided communities and dissolved morality bears some resemblance to the fear of the metropolitan slum exploding during communal and ethnic tensions nowadays.

However, there is a crucial difference. Underneath this fearsome memory of villages exploding in violence is the image of a village, pristine in its ability to reconcile—in fact celebrate—differences, even when that difference is tinged with caste hierarchy and principles of purity and pollution.[67] One remarkable and consistent part of the memories is the fondness and affection with which the survivors remember their multi-ethnic, multi-religious villages. In the context of Indian popular cinema, Chidananda Dasgupta talks of the village that ceases to be real in the life of the immigrant and turns into a dream. The dream is only sullied by the presence of the villain who has to be defeated at the end by the hero.[68] Time and the experience of pain has evidently brought about a different order of 'dream work' into the memory of the victims of Partition

[66] Jeet Behn, in Mehra and Pajiar, 'Sufferers and Survivors'.

[67] The reality during 1946–8 was more ambiguous. Going to the city as part of a rural mob to rob and kill in the city was not rare. Pandey talks about it in his 'Partition and Independence', p. 2264. So do a number of others. It is also a key imagery in a famous short story, Saadat Hassan Manto, 'Cold Meat', in Alok Bhalla (ed.), *Partition Stories* (New Delhi: HarperCollins, 1997), pp. 91–6.

[68] Chidananda Dasgupta, *The Painted Face: Studies in India's Popular Cinema* (New Delhi: Roli Books, 1991), p. 13.

violence. They have gone beyond the fantasy life of the consumers of popular cinema. Only in some cases is the villain re-discovered, not in the remembered village, but in life outside—in the form of a generic category called the Muslim, the Sikh, or the Hindu. Usually, it would appear that, over the years, all struggle, suffering, and conflicts have been painstakingly erased from the village of the mind. Above all, there is no communal tension in the remembered pre-Partition villages. Along with an easy life, prosperity (which usually means the availability of cheap foodstuff and articles of daily use), and cultural riches, the village as a pastoral paradise offers a perfect community life.[69]

To realists of all hues such nostalgic invocation of the village is a dangerous myth. It misleads one about the past and romanticizes what have always been ambivalent, if not hostile, social relations. To those to whom the denial of psychological realities is itself an index of objectification and authoritarianism, the victim's imagination of the pre-Partition village has an entirely different meaning. It looks like a crucial means of coping with post-traumatic stress. It reorders the memory of a journey that constantly threatens to take control of one's life; it reiterates the ethics of everyday life and multi-cultural living. Resorting to an idyllic past may be the survivors' way of relocating their journey through violence in a universe of memory that is less hate-filled, less buffeted by rage and dreams of revenge. Survivors remember their victimhood, they live with the trauma; they even re-do in their mind the journey across the border, marking the end of innocence; even the ill-treatment and brutalization at the end of the journey in strange cities, refugee camps, in new vocational situations. Nonetheless, some semblance of restoration of a moral universe is

[69] Cf. Dipesh Chakrabarty, 'Remembered Villages: Representation of Hindu–Bengali Memories in the Aftermath of the Partition', *Economic and Political Weekly*, August 10, 1996, pp. 2143–51; and Pandey, 'Partition and Independence'.

possible in the memory of the village from which one has been exiled and the memory of a culture to which one should be loyal. I have already argued that the village at one plane, is the ultimate prototype of Indian civilization and serves not merely as a critique of the city, but also as the anchor of virtually all traditional visions of a desirable lifestyle.

At the same time, potentially, Partition violence becomes in the memory an interplay of two forces—the village that was contaminated or poisoned and the city that regurgitated the poison that was already within it. The city of the imagination had already turned mildly pathological during the colonial times; it was no longer the city of classical Sanskrit plays, medieval trade centres, or pilgrimages. It now symbolized the loss of neighbourhood and community, combined with greed, amoral individualism, and ruthlessness. Its seductiveness was now tinged with a certain sinfulness and the scope to act out one's private fantasies by living at the margins of or outside conventions and norms. Partition marked the end of innocence because the journey to the new city could no longer be imagined as only a self-propelled one, a product of one's personal whimsy or capitulation to temptation. One could now be forced to abandon one's village home and pushed wholesale into a foreign city. One might even be in a situation where an alien city becomes one's saviour.

If one lived in a city in pre-Partition days and not in a village, the image of the city has been split. For those uprooted, the memory of the abandoned city has acquired—especially if they come from addictive cities like Lahore, Calcutta, Delhi, Dhaka, Lucknow, Hyderabad—some of the features of the remembered village and shed some of the traits that made them antonyms of the village. The memory continues to haunt the victim despite the passage of time. However, that is not the whole story. On another plane, the city that gave one shelter has become witness to one's humiliating, forced integration into an anonymous mass. This other city of the mind is the one where one became a worker or a professional, where one ceased to have a vocation or occupy a unique, culturally identifiable space as an artisan or craftsperson. On this plane, the city that gave one refuge took away one's cultural location, only to give one a stereotyped cultural image. For, being a refugee also often made one part of a recognizable, usually endogamous, caste-like group, identified with pushy, entrepreneurial go-getting and cutting corners.

It is perhaps not strange that, for many survivors, the country that was declared their official abode and provided them with a safe haven has still remained a foreign land. Unbelievably, after fifty years, almost all respondents—in India, Pakistan, and Bangladesh—talked of the abandoned village or city as their homeland, and their adopted land as someone else's country. For Sindhi Hindus, for instance, as I have pointed out, their migration from Sindh has now come to mean not merely the loss of culture but also the loss of a part of their religious heritage, particularly those traditions that they shared with Sindhi Muslims but not with non-Sindhi Hindus.[70]

Such imageries ensure that, to the survivors, the violence in 1946–8 remains a partly unexplained chapter of their lives and times. For most there was in the riots a touch of the principle of violence-for-the-sake-of-violence—a necrophilia, the presence of which they tacitly admit. They place their experiences outside the range of normality, sanity, and even comprehensibility. Perhaps that is their way of coping with trauma. It makes the return to normality slightly easier for many.

[70] This could be more true of refugees who came to India than of those who went to Pakistan. For the latter, the term *watan*, homeland, is double-edged—'the watan is *in* India but is *not* India'. Khan, 'Identity, Violence and Women', pp. 158–9.

VI

SETTLING SCORES

The violence ended in the winter of 1947–8, rather unexpectedly. It ended not through state intervention but, one suspects, through sheer tiredness and the sense of the futility of it all. The assassination of Gandhi at the hands of a Hindu fanatic on 30 January 1948 also played a role. Instead of weakening the forces of tolerance and amity, it strengthened them. Gandhi had walked through the riot-devastated villages of Noakhali with results that could only be called moving and the effects of his 'fast unto death' to stop the carnage at Delhi was said to be 'electric'. Muslims at Delhi talked of his arrival as rain after a particularly long and harsh summer, for afterwards no major riot took place in the city.[71] His fast not only brought peace, but also a new self-awareness. Pandey reports that M.S. Randhawa, the notoriously partisan deputy commissioner of police at Delhi, 'even took a group of Hindu and Sikh leaders to begin repairs to the shrine of the Sufi saint Khwaja Qutubuddin Bakhtiar Chishti, near Mehrauli, which had been desecrated.'[72] The fast had also revealed that though the infant states of India and Pakistan were born in hatred, Gandhi's moral stature still cut across the new borders. During the fast 'there were anxious enquiries about Gandhi's health even from across the borders and officers and ministers in the Pakistan government sought for ways to offer him support.'[73] The Muslim League, otherwise a bitter opponent of Gandhi, passed a resolution expressing its 'deep sense of appreciation' for his efforts.[74]

However, Gandhi could not be everywhere and, by the end of January 1948, he was in any case dead. How did the people and

[71] Pandey, 'Partition and Independence', p. 2266.

[72] Ibid., p. 2264.

[73] Ibid.

[74] Dilip Simeon, 'The Futility of Commonsense: An Essay on Ahimsa', *The Eye*, October–December 1997, 5 (1), pp. 15–23; see p. 20.

communities caught in the web of violence return from their journey into madness? Why did peace suddenly descend in north India? Does that uncertain return have anything to say about South Asian cultures and personality and their complex inter-relationship? In the end, I shall touch upon this issue with the help of a real-life parable, a news story reported in *The Statesman*, the Calcutta daily. To transcend the past, the parable suggests, one need not always museumize, whitewash, objectify or exorcize it; one can live with it and yet exercise principled forgetfulness.[75]

Meharbanpura was a Muslim-dominated village at the time of Partition and when the exodus of the Muslims from the surrounding villages began, a few thousand got together and camped in Meharbanpura. Around this camp were villages dominated by the Sikhs and the Hindus. Hardial Kaur, a villager now in her 80s, re-collects: 'Mutual distrust between the Sikhs and the Hindus on one side and the Muslims on the other was the order of the day. The flames of distrust were fuelled not only by authentic inform-ation of communal clashes but also by rumours about each side having acquired *asla* [ammunition] and that major strikes were being planned by the fanatics on both sides.'[76] Daljeet Singh, another elderly villager, continues the story. A couple of days after Independence in 1947, a mob of about 200 people from the Sikh and Hindu-dominated villages planned an attack on the Muslim camp in Meharbanpura. The attack was to be led by Bhan Singh, known to be a fanatic. Another resident adds, 'Bhan Singh had been planning an attack for a number of days, had obtained some

[75] Ashis Nandy, 'History's Forgotten Doubles', *History and Theory*, 1995, 34 (2), pp. 44–66.

[76] 'Romance in the Days of Partition', *The Statesman*, 6 August 1997.

weapons from Amritsar and had provoked and persuaded the non-Muslim residents into attacking the Muslim camp to drive away the occupants.'[77] According to Daljeet Singh, who saw the events from a distance, 'the Muslims in the camp who numbered over 2,000 apparently got to know of the attack and were well prepared to face it. Unfortunately for Bhan Singh, the . . . rifle he was carrying, failed him and after a brief skirmish outside the Muslim camp at Meharbanpura, most of his associates fled while he was overpowered and brutally done to death.'[78]

Bhan Singh's daughter-in-law, Palo, still stays in the village. She picks up the thread of the story. Bhan Singh's son Harbans Singh, she says, was posted as a head constable at Jhabbal in the Khem Karan area. During the course of his duty, he found a helpless young Muslim woman, Nawab Bibi, whose immediate family had been murdered, and the whereabouts of her other relatives were not known. 'As she was helpless,' Palo says, 'we gave her shelter and she was apparently reconciled to staying here.'[79]

However, the official process of repatriation of women who had been kept in captivity on both sides of the border started after the bloodshed had stopped. According to Palo, 'Some person harbouring animosity towards our family informed the authorities and some officials came in early 1949 and took away Nawab Bibi in the absence of Harbans Singh.'

Harbans looked for her at the border and in government offices, but failed. Finally, after a few weeks, he assumed the name Barkat Ali and arranged to cross the border into Pakistan by paying a middle-man the princely sum of Rs 30. In Lahore, under his new name, Harbans produced some papers to show that he was a displaced Muslim from Sultanwind area on the outskirts of Amritsar. He was allotted two shops in a village near Lahore and he

[77] Ibid.
[78] Ibid.
[79] Ibid.

started a cloth business. According to *The Statesman*, 'He kept trying to trace his "beloved" and . . . managed to find her. The list of names of those displaced was available with the authorities and this apparently helped Harbans trace Nawab Bibi.'[80]

The newspaper does not tell us if Barkat Ali, *alias* Harbans Singh, son of the feared Sikh fanatic Bhan Singh, and Nawab Bibi, the victimized Muslim woman whose whole family had died at the hands of the Sikhs, lived happily ever afterwards. But frankly I would like to believe that they do.

[80] Ibid.

Index